Billeted in STROUD 1939–40

AN EVACUEE'S ACCOUNT

Stroud
and THE COTSWOLDS

Billeted in STROUD 1939–40

AN EVACUEE'S ACCOUNT

ERIC ARMSTRONG

AMBERLEY

This book has been written for several reasons: the author's pleasure recalling, in some detail, life in Stroud during 1939/40, part of an answer to the question 'what did you do in the war, Dad, Granddad, Great Granddad', a celebration of the seventieth (plus a bit) anniversary of my loss of evacuee status and, what I hope will be regarded as, a mostly complimentary description of Stroud and its environment as I experienced life there as a stranger. In an oblique way, the work forms a genuine and hearty 'thank you' for arguably the most carefree period of my life. While a lengthy preliminary autobiography would be out of place, some knowledge of my life to the age of sixteen might help the reader to understand more readily, why I saw the world as I did.

First published 2011

Amberley Publishing Plc
Cirencester Road, Chalford,
Stroud, Gloucestershire, GL6 8PE

www.amberleybooks.com

Copyright © Eric Armstrong 2011

The right of Eric Armstrong to be identified as the Author
of this work has been asserted in accordance with the
Copyrights, Designs and Patents Act 1988.

British Library Cataloguing in Publication Data.
A catalogue record for this book is available from the British Library.

ISBN 978-1-4456-0293-6

Typeset in 10pt on 12pt Sabon.
Typesetting and Origination by Amberley Publishing.
Printed in the UK.

Contents

Chapter 1

1923-1939

In 1923 I was born at home, by gaslight, in Handsworth, Birmingham, the youngest of six children and the only child of my father's second marriage. My eldest half-brother Harold, an artillery gunner was killed in France a few months before the guns fell silent in November 1918. My other half-brothers Les and Jack served with the Royal Flying Corps.

My background, like that of many a contemporary lad and lass, could conventionally be categorised as humble. Not the humble of instilled deference or the monstrous hypocrisy of a Uriah Heep, but the humble used as a euphemism for 'straitened circumstances'. By those words I mean the constant grinding struggle by honest toilers to pay the rent, to keep clean in properties lacking bathrooms and piped hot water, and with toilets in the backyard entailing a night time regime of chamber-pot use. 'Slopping out' was not the monopoly of the prison population.

My boyhood was reasonably happy. But I became aware of and puzzled by differences between myself and some of my school pals. Take brothers Harry and Stephen for instance, who always had many more 'lead soldiers' than I had – a company of several dozen, in good order compared to my handful of skirmishing, battle scarred irregulars. Harry and Stephen went with their parents for summer holidays by the sea. Similarly, brothers John and Trevor went to Cromer every year. My once in a while treat was to spend a day or two with aunts at their homes in the Black Country with the company of what seemed a myriad of good natured cousins.

There were times when I felt quite lonely. One by one, my brothers left the family home to establish homes for themselves. My father was in and out of hospital for a total of several months. To keep the wolf from the door, my mother took on charring work including hard scrubbing and cleaning in the evenings at a dairy in Aston. Eventually, Dad came home awkwardly swinging a gammy right leg, permanently stiff from the operation for osteomyelitis. Penicillin had yet to be discovered. Thankfully amputation had been averted, but handicapped as he now was, Dad found it hard to find regular work. Mom exchanged dairy work for looking after her father, now a widower, and her two bachelor brothers.

In 1934 came a sea change. At the council school in Westminster Road I did sufficiently well to gain a place at the Handsworth Grammar School for Boys in Grove Lane. To my bewilderment I found I had entered an unfamiliar, even slightly weird world where subjects, like algebra were taught for some abstruse reason and where some teachers talked of 'plarnts' and 'carstles'. All the teachers swished

20. My father is a partaker of glory at present, Master Copperfield, but we have much to be thankful for.

Left: David Copperfield's Uriah Heep.

Below: Dad swinging a leg and Eric wearing 'Brummagem gloves' in Corporation Street, Birmingham *c.* 1929.

Uncle George and Eric, Torquay 1937.

around in long black gowns of office which increased their distance from the young boys. For a year or two, like other lads from similar backgrounds, I floundered. No one at home could help me academically yet I persevered, partly out of fear, doing well enough to gain a form prize each year.

Then in 1937, it was probably exchanging short for long trousers that did it, at fourteen I began to enter, if not a comfort zone, then a zone of greater self-confidence and enjoyment. Associated with that feeling was the joy and memories of a real summer holiday, for two whole weeks, at Babbacombe, Devon, where I experienced my first sight of the sea!

My benefactors were the two uncles mentioned earlier. Arthur and George were bachelors and for the most part left me to my own devices. But they did take me to Kent Cavern and Buckfast Abbey, as well as Cockington village. Although targeted by the comely widowed landlady, Uncle Arthur escaped unscathed and I learned something of 'wimmen's' wiles and ways. At the time of course, the ambition of most women was to achieve married status. Some of those who did not succeed regarded themselves as failures. 'On the shelf' was the conventional term.

On returning to school in September I felt I was passing from boy to youth – not fully fledged in masculine matters but excitingly on the way. And so 1938 turned out to be a great year, even if war clouds were beginning to build in ominous fashion.

After gaining the important School Certificate, I moved with various pals from form VC into the Lower Sixth. Farewell to fiendish algebra, boring geometry, physics, chemistry, geography. Now I could tackle with greater commitment, English, History, French and German. 'Yippee!' as the diary entry has it.

HGS, Handsworth Grammar School, Grove Lane.

I went on to play regularly at left back for the Second XI at football, becoming the captain and occasionally playing for the First XI. And I also fell in love! Yippee once again.

The highly attractive and greatly popular Margaret was fourteen when we met by chance, but not on one of the so-called 'monkey-runs' of Birchfield Road, Soho Road or Lozells Road where young 'guys and dolls', usually in pairs, strolled up and down of an evening, seeking to make suitable acquaintances for desirable dates.

Our romance blossomed, yet stayed within the boundaries of the conventions set for youthful courtship. We exchanged our first kisses under discreet but indulgent parental supervision by means of the party kissing game of 'Postman's Knock,' always popular at Christmas time. Margaret, to my delight, was something of a tomboy fully prepared to walk with me through parks, fields and bluebell woods, in every type of weather. We went regularly together to the pictures and Margaret stood for hours with me in a quagmire pelted by nearly unceasing cold rain at the opening of Birmingham's municipal airport at Elmdon on 8 July 1939. Inevitably perhaps, we quarrelled (not over ruined shoes) and parted. But a link of connection still held as this book will show.

*

In the meantime, a relevant digression on then and now might be of help in understanding a little better, life in the 1930s.

Let us suppose that a small group of perceptive teenagers of today could travel back in time to a yesterday of the late 1930s. What differences might they spot in a typical, small-terraced house of three bedrooms?

The two-seater monoplanes bearing RAF roundels are probably trainers, at Elmdon.

Starting in a cramped and cluttered kitchen, the following might catch their eyes: lead pipes to deliver the water supply (but no piped hot water), a shallow brownstone sink, a bricked in coal fired metal boiler for Monday's washing toil, a heavy iron mangle, a wooden 'safe' with metal mesh to keep the mackerel fresh, a roller towel on the back of the door to the yard and a gas cooker. Moving into the living room they'd see chipped second hand furniture, an open fireplace, a mantelpiece, a coal scuttle and fire-irons, a toasting fork, linoleum (cracked here and there) covering the floor, one or two small rugs (possibly home-made); on a well polished dresser, a wireless with its accoutrements of wires, battery and accumulator, possibly a wind-up gramophone, powered by a steel spring, some dinner plate sized records made of that curious black material known as shellac, designed to turn at 78 revolutions per minute (hence 78 rpm) and few, if any, electric sockets. The front room, or parlour, was similar to the living room but with its fireplace seldom used, except perhaps a fire blazing in the grate at Christmas time. Above, on the wall, the framed portrait of a young soldier, smiling, who had gone to war. On the stairs would be a well worn narrow carpet, possibly held in place by metal stair-rods. Now for the bedrooms: an empty fireplace in each, an empty chamber-pot under each bed, sash windows (downstairs as well). At first floor level, sash windows were not always cleaned by paid cleaners but sometimes by the lady of the house, in floral pinafore, who would slide the lower pane up to join the upper pane. The resultant aperture allowed the cleaner to wriggle the upper part of her body into the open air and to sit on the sill with her back to the street and away she would go, removing some of the city's grime and making sure her windows were at least as sparkling as those of her neighbours. In the amiable way ladies have, some of them would synchronise their cleaning and enjoy a bit of a chat.

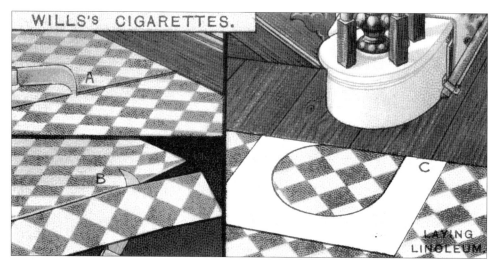

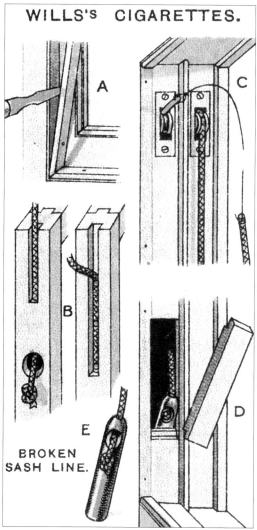

Above: 1930s Lino.

Left: The Sash window, typical style of the age.

Right: A Birmingham scene from 1954, with sash windows much in evidence.

Below: Four wheeled bread vans were also a common sight, being favoured by the larger bakers such as the Co-op.

Ernest Bevin, an eminent trade union leader and prominent figure in the Labour movement, was appointed by Winston Churchill in 1940 to the arduous post of Minister of Labour and National Service.

ASTON VILLA F.C.
CHAMPIONS DIV II, 1937–38

The team that won promotion to the First Division.

B.C.S. Butchery Display.
B.C.S. Jubilee Exhibition 1931

The Birmingham Co-operative Society celebrated its Golden Jubilee in 1931, partly with an extensive display of its many and varied activities. Our membership number was 20822. The Co-op divvy was a godsend for many working class families.

Of course, there could be the occasional catcall from a passing urchin or a cheeky remark from a coalman. In the backyard our observers would spot the amount of coal in the coalhouse and bundles of firewood, some of them bound with wire as today. In the lavatory, the seat usually boarded in, could be found the news of last week, spiked on a bent nail, in the form of newspapers torn into squares, fit for their particular purpose. The cistern was joined to a lead pipe which, after a spell of hard frost could split and with a thaw cause a variety of watery problems. In the road, our observers would be struck not by the volume of cars and lorries but of horse-drawn traffic, bread vans, milk floats and coal carts. Horses left their calling cards at random. These were handy for the householder growing rhubarb in his tiny back-garden.

So, what would our teenagers miss most if they were trapped in a 1930's time warp? Almost certainly the following 'necessities';

A TV, a bath, a shower, a fridge, central heating, hot water on tap, electricity supply with plenty of sockets, a microwave oven, an electric toaster, an electric kettle, washing machine, drier, dish washer, a computer, mobile and static phones, an indoor toilet with toilet rolls and tissues, carpets ... the list could become a long one but almost certainly would not include carbolic soap.

*

In its way, the above comparison serves as a reminder of how relatively primitive, in some material regards, life was seventy odd years ago. That assessment would not apply to social behaviour but perhaps more about that later.

To sum up, by and large our family and many of our neighbours followed three guiding stars: Vote Labour, Support Aston Villa, shop at the Co-op.

Chapter 2
August, September and October 1939

As the end of August approached, it became overwhelmingly self-evident that in a few days time we would be at war with Germany. Consequently, the government set in motion operation 'Pied Piper', a plan that had never before been devised, let alone attempted i.e. the mass evacuation of children and some adults from cities and towns thought to be potential targets for enemy bombers.

A splendid book of description, explanation and analysis of the whole process and experience has been written by James Roffey, titled *Send Them to Safety*. (Evacuees Reunion Association, 2009).

But for me things were not as straightforward as I wished them to be. What follows are relevant excerpts from my diaries, with explanatory comments given in square brackets.

Thursday 31
Kids supposed to evacuate this afternoon. Later told that it is tomorrow. Said goodbye to John and all my pals. May never see them again. [That last sentence may sound excessively lugubrious as if Hitler had made a bomb with my name on it. Not so, it simply meant that while these sixth formers might be capering around Stroud I might have become a wage slave in some grubby office.] John, Sharpley and Merriman going to write. Shall have to go to work if Education Committee will let me.

[In short, I was in limbo. Evacuation was not compulsory but parents were strongly urged by the government to send their children to safer places. Apparently, more than 30,000 Brummie children were expected to become evacuees. 351 Handsworth Grammar School boys and 26 teachers and helpers entrained for Stroud. This meant that more than 200 boys had to settle for involuntary playing the wag for as yet, an unknown period of time.

In my own case, the reference to the Education Committee resulted from a metaphorical head-on collision between Mom and Dad about my future. My father, born in 1878 left school, like his contemporaries, at the age of 12. Dad was not the stern, stereotypical Victorian disciplinarian. He held liberal to socialist views and wrote a good hand. He simply thought that I had now received sufficient schooling to get a decent clerical job and so ease our chronic money worries.

My mother, I believed, had once cherished hopes of becoming a school-ma'm herself but was thwarted by harsh family circumstances.

She held the view that I would get a still better job if I stayed on at school for one more year and gained my Higher School Certificate in the summer of 1940. I shared my mother's view but it was for the Committee to decide.

From the outset in 1934, this Committee had made a quite generous maintenance grant to my parents for my grammar school attendance and performance. A payment had already been made for the Autumn Term of 1939, a term with many unknowns.

On the 3 September, a Sunday, Britain duly declared war on Germany. My diary records that anti-aircraft guns were already manned in Perry Barr Park, barrage balloons were in place on a field adjoining our school playing field, and a complete black-out was in force at night. Like the rest of the nation I said, 'Now I wonder what will happen'.

Apprehension, not fear, permeated the atmosphere. Air raids were widely expected and the use of poisonous gas was held to be a real possibility, hence the issue of gas masks to every single person. Two of my uncles, one from each side of the family, had been gassed in the First World War. One died prematurely in the 1920s, the other survived, on one lung, well past the end of the Second World War.

During this period of fretful waiting, I occupied my time by walking a great deal, mainly through parks and along a canal, whittling wood, reading a *Short History of French Literature*, just in case. Then, on 7 September I was immensely cheered up by a letter from Herbert Sharpley and a postcard from John Archer – from Stroud!

Here are a few pertinent excerpts from the letter. For some arcane schoolboy reason we seldom addressed one another by Christian names. Herbert became Syd and I was Alf].

Dear Alf,

Well here we are in Stroud ... so far everything has been great ... The billets are very comfortable but due the straggling nature of the town they are about ¾ of a mile from the school. This is quite a decent place the older part is in stone but the majority of the form rooms etc is wooden & rather temporary looking. The hall is very nice & has a gallery, also seats which fortunately are just numerous enough to seat the whole of our crowd i.e. about 400.

Stroud itself is a very nice town but there are hills, hills, hills & then some hills. [No doubt accurate but a tad terse, jejune in fact. Now that's a word seldom seen or heard – jejune. Ah, the benefits of a grammar school education.] One walks for a few yards then suddenly seems to ascend vertically upwards, having proceeded thus for a breathless ¼ of a mile you are suddenly aware of that sinking feeling & a precipitous descent awaits the unwary. [Clearly this lad has the makings of a navigator which he subsequently became in the RAF]. The country is marvellous & so far we have spent the afternoons and evenings walking around the neighbouring boigs*. We have been to school one or two mornings but only to show Billy Peck** that we have not done a sudden decease in the night. Tomorrow however we sally forth to dig trenches, national defence and all that you know, so think of me wielding a deft pick & deftly picking my way to Australia.

[* boig – thought to have been picked up from American gangster films, meaning a town or district. ** Peck was the nickname of one of the senior masters. May derive from the shape of his nose and curious jerks of the head.]

All Communications to be addressed to THE CHIEF EDUCATION OFFICER.

CITY OF BIRMINGHAM
EDUCATION DEPARTMENT
COUNCIL HOUSE, MARGARET ST.
BIRMINGHAM 3

P. D. INNES, C.B.E., M.A., D. Sc.,
Chief Education Officer.

Telephone:
CENTRAL 7000

Dear Sir, or Madam,　　　HE/2/B.　　　24th June, 193 8.

| Pupil Eric G.A. Armstrong. | Office Record No. 34/7 |
| School Handsworth Grammar School. | |

to be quoted in all communications to the Office.

I have to inform you that the following award (or revised award), has been made to the above-named pupil in accordance with the terms and conditions of the Committee's Scheme. It is subject to satisfactory attendance, progress and conduct and will be reviewed from to time.

School Fees	Maintenance Allowance	To Date	Basis of Assessment
Full Exemption (Fees payable at the rate of £ Nil per annum). See note (1) overleaf.	At the rate of £ 20. 0. 0. per annum. (Increased from £15) See note (2) overleaf.	From September 193 8 To July, 193 9	Return of Income for year ended 31st March last. 1 dependent child(ren). 1 child(ren) undergoing an approved course of full time higher education.

In the event of any alteration in the number of dependent children (*i.e.* children under 14 or any over 14 undergoing full-time education), an alteration in the number of children undergoing an approved course of full time higher education as defined in the Scheme, or your removal to an address outside the City Boundary, you are required to notify me immediately. As the Committee reserve the right to adjust awards retrospectively on these counts, failure to send in proper notification will result in your being called upon to pay any sum due to the Committee as the result of such retrospective adjustment.

Mr. A.J. Armstrong,

37 Hutton Road,

Handsworth,

BIRMINGHAM.

FOR NOTES SEE OVER.

Yours faithfully,

P.D. Innes

Chief Education Officer.

P59093

Confirmation of my maintenance grant.

BALLOON BARRAGE

Barrage balloons were a common sight near densley populated areas.

WILL'S CIGARETTES

THE CIVILIAN RESPIRATOR—HOW TO ADJUST IT

Everyone was issued with a gas-mask.

WILLS'S CIGARETTES

ANTI-AIRCRAFT GUN

Anti-aircraft guns aided the RAF's struggle against the Luftwaffe.

The only snag so far is that we all have to be in our billets by 7.30 but successful evasions of masters have been carried out by nipping out up another street. Peck tried to scoot round & see us all on Friday night at our billets as arranged but nearly broke his neck as there was a black out in progress. Hope you are getting on OK. Yours etc Syd. The address is S Johnson, 1, Stratton Villas, Slad Road, Stroud, Glos.

9 *Saturday*

Had a letter from John Archer this morning. He is billeted with Lowe. Been digging trenches for 2 days. [Lest it be thought that only Handsworth Grammar School senior boys had been drafted into a civilian Pioneer Corps, it is on record that boys from Central School, Stroud had been doing similar work.]

Our new school, Marling, in Stroud.

13 Wednesday
Walked to the Beacon cinema in the afternoon since it is allowed to open as it is in a neutral area. Saw *The Son of Frankenstein*.

14 Thursday,
Hooray! Lots of cheers. Had a letter from Margaret. She is at Worcester. Very friendly letter.

16 Saturday
... pictures ... reopened everywhere yesterday ... Seems a funny war. We are told so very little. [Because of expected air raids, the government, at the out-break of war had decreed that all places of entertainment should be closed 'until further notice.' The importance of entertainment to public morale was soon acknowledged and the sanction relaxed.]

18 Monday
Air raid shelter arrived this morning. [Dad was furious and would not accept delivery of the corrugated metal sheets (free to us on low income). He gave no clear reasons why. I can only think he would rather stay in bed during an air raid than suffer the indignity of being lifted in and out of the Anderson shelter because of his stiff leg. He knew full well that our next door neighbours, the mild mannered Stanleys would let Mom and I share their shelter when the time came, which is what happened.]

✻

The School Hall.

Slad Road, Stroud.

Immediately after Mr. Chamberlain's dramatic broadcast to the nation, the Government yesterday announced a number of precautionary measures to prevent people crowding together and so increasing the casualty risks from air raids.

Instructions were given for the closing of all places of entertainment until further notice. In the light of experience it may be possible to open cinemas and theatres in some areas later. Included in the closure orders are indoor and outdoor sports gatherings where large numbers of people might be expected to congregate.

The following advice is given :—

Keep off the streets as much as possible ; to expose yourself unnecessarily adds to your danger.

Carry your gas mask with you always.

Make sure every member of your household have on them their names and addresses clearly written. Do this on an envelope or luggage label and not on an odd piece of paper which may be lost.

Sew a label on children's clothing so that they cannot pull it off.

People are requested not to crowd together unnecessarily in any circumstances.

Churches and other places of public worship will not be closed.

All day schools in evacuation and neutral areas in England, Wales and Scotland are to be closed for lessons for at least a week from yesterday.

In the reception areas schools will be opened as soon as evacuation is complete.

Cinemas, Theatres Close to Cut Risks

Precautions were taken to act against the heavy casualties incurred when people gathered together.

[War events continued to be entered in my diary. Some were not of startling interest or importance but some were: the never ceasing battle against the German U Boats, the conquest of Poland and its division between Germany and Russia, the introduction of food rationing, an Emergency Budget, sugar up a penny a pound, beer up by a penny a pint.

Activities began to stir on the Home Front, people seeking to restore as much normal life as possible. A few old chums who had left school or were at a loss at home like myself made plans to form a football team.

October arrived:]

Saturday 7
Had a P.C. from Junevile Labour Employment Bureau this morning. Only to tell me might have to refund Maintainance money already received or be evacuated. Matter to go before a committee. [Did the spelling mistakes result from wartime stress? Balderdash! One arose from a genuine misunderstanding and the other constituted a touch of schoolboy facetious humour. While I fretted and waited, I re-read Syd's letter received on 7 September and a letter from a teacher.]

Frank G Gaydoul   c/o Jack Smith Esq.,
                                  Morningside

                         Rodborough Avenue

                         Stroud Glos.

                         5th October 1939

Dear Armstrong,

                Many thanks for that precious parcel,
which is a great help. Enclosed 6d in stamps for your
postage.

    We are all right down here enjoying the country air
scenery and half day school. One boy on my beat has
put on ten pounds already,That shows you what the rest
does for us. We are all good boys and go to church on
Sundays.More boys are coming down here regularly and and
an equal number are going home regularly.Why don't you
join us and learn fishing?There's a new Society the Fishing
Club-qualifications   strong imagination & indisposition
to take a healthy part in games.TWO more have been
invented but I don't know their exact names.One collects K
Konkers & the other steals apples(when the farmer isn't
lookin)There are lots of simply lovely girls here.all sorts
and sizes.Archer will tell you about that....

    Must close now with best thanks,

                Gott straf' Hitler !   Frank G Gaydoul

I perhaps wondered fleetingly how this teacher of German came to know about Stroud
girls, but at the time I was a one gal guy.

By the way I don't know whether you are aware that this boig owns a park, quite a nice one too complete with swimming pool, putting green and si sur. [A sort of franglais for see-saw] ...certainly missing your visage au souris [smiling face] at the Marling edifice. The lates are going great guns, they consider it an off day if at least 40 clients attend. It looks like a second assembly when they have detention ... Yours...Syd.

[At Handsworth Grammar School the two of us, self-conscious in short black gowns of prefect office, had been detailed to stand at the school entrance when assembly in the hall started, to record latecomers who then stood in line in a corridor nearby. The challenge was to check the validity of excuses made. Did the chain really come off the bike? Was the excuse note written in a grown up or younger hand? As the line of 'miscreants' lengthened, the hubbub increased – and we were then reprimanded, on occasion, by higher authority.]

14 Saturday
Battleship *Royal Oak* sunk believed by submarine action. [A savage set-back. This veteran battleship was at anchor in thought to be virtually invulnerable Scapa Flow. More than 800 sailors perished.]

16 Monday
First air attack on Britain ... Rosyth naval base and Forth Bridge.

18 Wednesday
Had to go after a job this morning London Aliminium Co. Witton. [Spelling mistake acknowledged.]

24 Tuesday
No reply yet Mom posted letter to Josef [not Stalin but the Reverend J. J. Walton, headmaster]. Hope he can find me a billet.

25 Wednesday
Reply from Education Committee. Have to pay £13 if I want to leave so I'm not leaving. Booked trip for Stroud. [Crisp and to the point.]

27 Friday
Had a reply from Jo, this morn. O.K. all fixed. [Jo] very pleased I am going.

28 Saturday
Played football in the park in the afternoon. We had a full team in full kit. [The earlier *ad hoc* arrangements were becoming fixtures.]

29 Sunday
Arrived at Stroud [by coach] ½ p 12 after travelling through beautiful country. Mr and Mrs Wheatley a very nice couple. Elderly but I feel confident that I shall be happy here. Good to see old Syd Sharpley again. Plenty of hills in Stroud. Played crib at night.

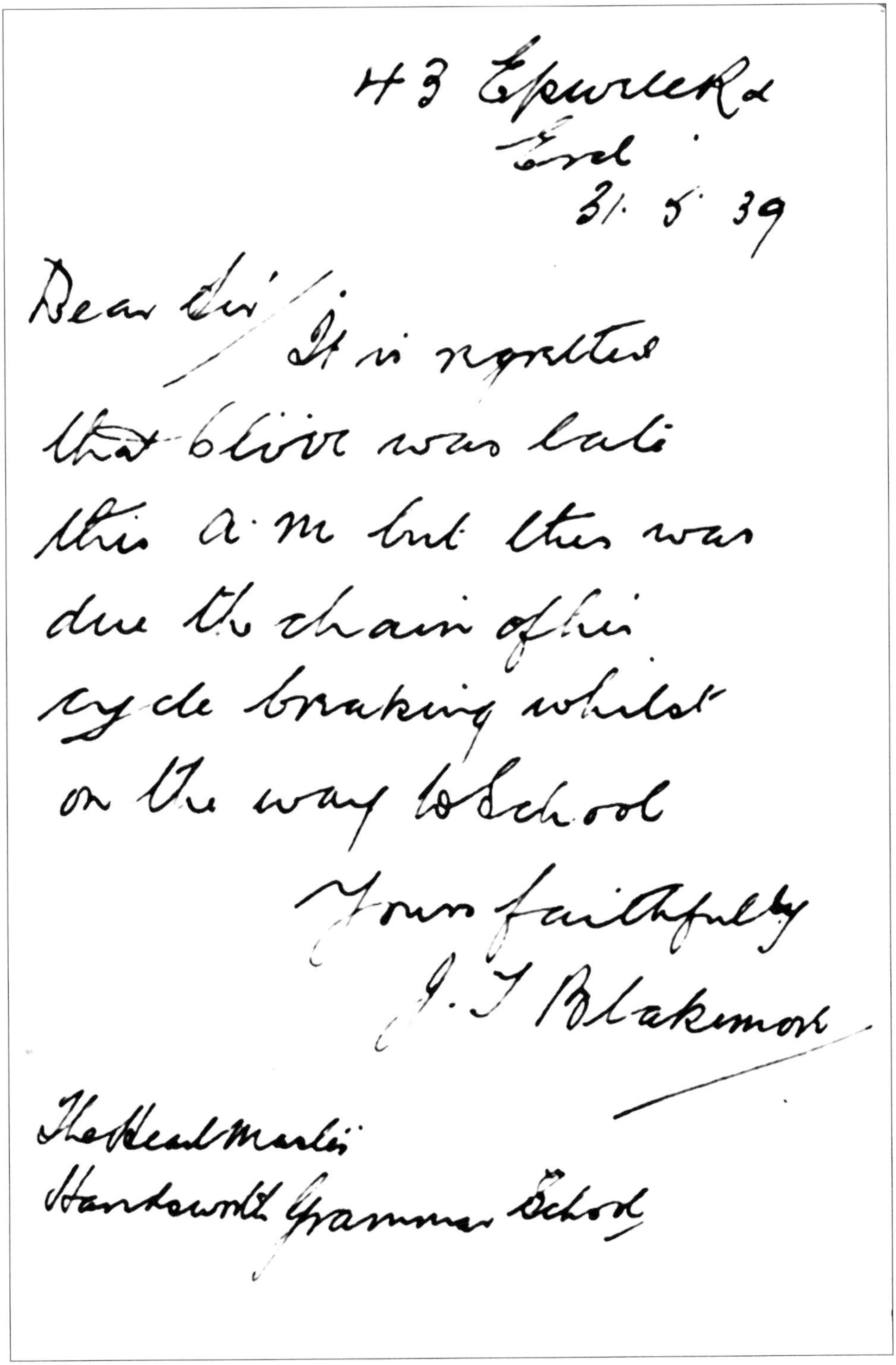

43 Epworth Rd

Erd

31. 5. 39

Dear Sir,

It is regretted that Clive was late this a.m but this was due the chain of his cycle breaking whilst on the way to School

Yours faithfully

J. T. Blakemore

The Head Master

Handsworth Grammar School

A classic ruse used by late-comers to try and avoid punishment.

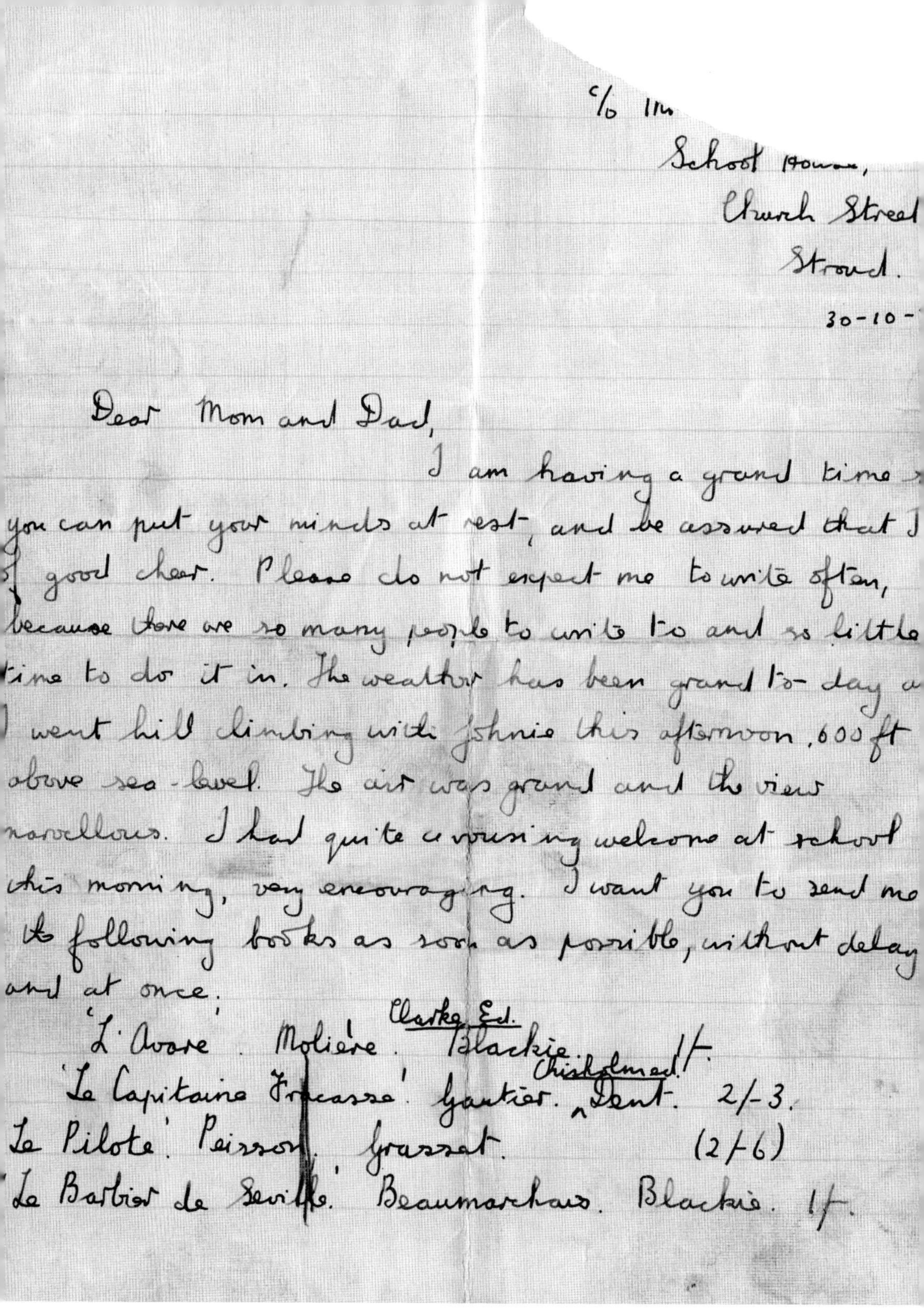

c/o Mrs
School House,
Church Street
Stroud.

30-10-

Dear Mom and Dad,

I am having a grand time, you can put your minds at rest, and be assured that I of good cheer. Please do not expect me to write often, because there are so many people to write to and so little time to do it in. The weather has been grand to-day a I went hill climbing with Johnie this afternoon, 600 ft above sea-level. The air was grand and the view marvellous. I had quite a rousing welcome at school this morning, very encouraging. I want you to send me the following books as soon as possible, without delay and at once;

'L'Avare'. Molière. Blackie. Clarke. Ed.
'Le Capitaine Fracasse' Gautier. Dent. Chisholm ed. 2/-3.
'Le Pilote'. Peisson. Grasset. (2/-6)
'Le Barbier de Séville'. Beaumarchais. Blackie. 1/-.

My first letter home from Stroud.

Advanced French Prose Composition. Duhamel.
Rivingtons.   5/-
'La France et les Français'   I've forgotten the
particulars about this one but as comprehensive book
as you can about French habits and customs as
possible. Be careful and make inquiries about this one.
"Coriolanus'. Shakespeare. New Hudson. Edition.| Most
"Hamlet".   "   "   " | Most
                                                          preferable

            Please get all these books as soon as you
possibly can. I should try Cornishes. If not Midland
Educational.
            Well I will close now as I have several
that letters to write.
                    Lots of love, remember me to everyone at
26 and Wellington Rd.
                    from your son,
                            Eric.
P.S. Send me a towel.

A *TREAT* in every bite and A *MEAL* in every bar

STILL

2ᵈ

Mars

Here's something to get your teeth into, and boy is it *good!* Bite through the creamy milk chocolate coating, through the generous buttery caramel layer, deep down into the malted-milk-and-egg centre. Good eh? And you bet it's good, for you, too! Not only a big delicious bar, but a tidy meal into the bargain — and bargain's the word

Mars, still going strong in 2011 was a favourite over seventy years ago.

*

[The following day I wrote my first letter home, featuring a list af French books and their prices. The tone may sound a touch peremptory, partly due to my schoolboy cocky age and partly due to the need to catch up with my studies. The hill referred to was Rodborough and 226 Westminster Road was the home of my maternal grandparents and those jolly bachelor uncles already mentioned. In Wellington Road lived the uncle who had been gassed in the First World War.

At this time, I was brim-full of excitement, contemplating what I regarded as an adventure. Fond of my parents and home as I was, I relished the prospect of becoming more independent, free to explore new surroundings, meet different people, to work and play hard. Football, running and PT were on the agenda. As a townie with a yen for fresh air, like my dad, I was ready to make the most of my time as a visitor to fine countryside. Then came a serious set-back.]

*

31 *Tuesday*
After playing football found that some-one had half-inched my purse which contained over 9 shillings for books. Reported my loss but doubt if I shall ever see that money again. [I had no suspicion of anyone.]

Chapter 3
November 1939

1 Wednesday
Borrowed Rigby minor's bike in the afternoon and went with Syd and Hemming to Gloucester. Not much time to look round.

2 Thursday
Head offered to lend me some money. Very nice of him. [Assistance declined].

3 Friday
Double rainbow. Beautiful picture with sun on trees after rain. Went for a ride on Hemming's bike through most beautiful country.

4 Saturday
Rode to Gloucester on Hemming's bike ... Syd and Johnnie* came. Made an extensive tour of the cathedral. Beautiful building. Truly marvellous place. Had a super hot bath and listened to Bandwagon. Excellent. [* John Archer and I had lived as young boys in the same road and started school together in 1928. We were both friends and friendly rivals. As Mr and Mrs Wheatley were caretakers of the adjoining school, we were never without fuel. More will be said about Bandwagon later.]

5 Sunday
...marvellous autumnal tints up Slad Road. Went on a short ride to Sheepscombe.

6 Monday
...cycled to Tewkesbury ... looked round the abbey and an old mill. Very interesting. Then cycled to Bredon and then on to Twyning. Very enjoyable day. [No, I was not slacking, wagging off school, playing truant or skiving but enjoying my half term break in my preferred way. Many boys had gone home to Brum. I had only been a week in Stroud.]

7 Tuesday
Cycled just to Slad this morning ... Colours in trees still marvellous. Started school again in the afternoon. Don't like the idea at all. Only advantage is that we can stop in bed a little longer in the mornings, thanks to the kindness of Mr & Mrs Wheatley. Bless 'em!

Gloucester's beautiful cathedral.

The picturesque village of Sheepscombe.

Apart from the traffic warden, this 1995 photograph of our billet, 'School House' is very much as I remember it from much earlier days.

Slad Valley, near Stroud.

Above: Tewkesbury High Street.

Right: Tewkesbury Abbey.

Fletchers Mill, Tewkesbury.

*

[Marling School shared their premises, their time and facilities with us in a praiseworthy, equitable manner. In one week Marling boys would attend school during mornings and HGS boys in the afternoons as above. The following week, we would swap over times and that pattern of weekly change would continue as the diaries record. Activities had to be designed for the six half days 'off' a week. These included organised walks, games in the gym and outdoors and, especially for sixth formers, homework, revising for exams and exploring the environment, town and country. Eventually, HGS scholars were lumbered with afternoons only for lessons. This made for boring and fretful classwork on Saturday afternoons, especially galling when bat could be heard smiting ball nearby.]

*

8 Wednesday
...medically examined ... overjoyed to hear that there was nothing wrong with my feet, so I can run & run & run. [For some reason, dark suspicions had arisen about the arches of my feet. The arches were rather shallow but still fit for the purpose indicated.]

9 Thursday
Attempt made on Hitler's life. [Sadly, unsuccessful. The bomb in the Burgerbraukeller in Munich exploded just after Hitler had left the beer cellar having made a typical ranting speech.]

Daily Express

WORLD'S LARGEST DAILY SALE

No. 12,315   Thursday, November 9, 1939   One Penny

.m. EDITION   A defiant shriek "I'm ready for a five-year war!" then—

ITLER ESCAPES EXPLOSION
N A BEER CELLAR

ROYAL OAK SCANDAL

Who was to blame? SEE OPINION, PAGE SIX

dead, 60 hurt: Reported ttempt with time-bomb

MR. CHURCHILL declared in the House of Commons yesterday:—
"Our struggle at sea will be long and unrelenting, but in the end

WE SHALL BREAK THEIR HEARTS!

"I feel after the ninth week of the war that so far as the sea is concerned—and the sea has often proved decisive in the end—we may cherish good hopes that all will be well."
Full report begins on Page Five.

Daily Express Naval Reporter

ONE of the five subsidiary channels into Scapa Flow was left insufficiently blocked. That is the incredible fact that stands out from yesterday's official explanation of the loss of the Royal Oak.

It is a solution of the mystery that no student of naval affairs considered possible.

The whole lesson of 1914 was that Scapa was vulnerable unless all channels but those actually used by the Fleet were completely blocked to all ships.

The two channels for the Fleet were guarded in the last war by nets, minefields, and electrical detectors. As the U-boats found when these were in place, it was not possible for a submarine to get in without the watchers knowing that it was near the channel.

To leave one of the lesser approaches incompletely blocked after six weeks of war was not taking a legitimate war risk. It was a gamble with the lives of the officers and men of the Home Fleet.

WHY THE DELAY?

It was obvious last autumn that Scapa might be needed as a war base at any moment, and the most immediate task was to ensure that the harbour was submarine-proof.

The secondary channels into the Flow could be completely closed at any time without causing difficulty to the small amount of traffic going in and out of Scapa.

It is an appalling thought that

MINUTES AFTER HIS SPEECH

NTY-SEVEN MINUTES AFTER HITLER ENDED A HYSTERICAL SPEECH IN THE JERGERBRAU BEER CELLAR AT MUNICH LAST NIGHT—A SPEECH IN WHICH HE THAT HE WAS READY FOR A FIVE-YEARS' WAR WITH BRITAIN—THE BUILDING

HAKEN BY AN EXPLOSION WHICH
SIX MEMBERS OF THE "OLD GUARD"
E NAZI PARTY, AND INJURED SIXTY
PEOPLE.
ITLER HAD ALREADY LEFT AND
NOT HURT. HE LEFT EARLIER THAN
RIGINALLY INTENDED AS HE
SUMMONED BACK TO BERLIN BY
TANT STATE BUSINESS.
he identities of the dead and injured are
own, it is officially stated, says the British
ed Press from Berlin this morning.
ice admitted that the explosion was due to an
ve body"—not to a defective boiler, as was
ed at first. The official statement says that the
was inspired by foreign agents, and a reward
00 has been offered for the discovery of the
ators.

THEY'RE STILL AT SIXES AND SEVENS

The thin dotted line between Black-out and Light on Kilburn High-road last night at six. Shops on the West Hampstead side are open now until seven o'clock. Those across the road, in Willesden, are "curfewed" at six. "It's like hating one blind eye, walking down that way," says Hilde Marchant on Page Seven.

BRUSSELS. Report from Henry Fast, Daily Express Correspondent

3 Kings | R.A.F. BAG

Hitler survives one of the several attempts made on his life during the war.

10 Friday
Hooray, hooray, hooray … the long awaited epistle from Margaret. Hasn't forgotten me, just darn opposite. Yippee!

11 Saturday
Armistice day seems a terrible mockery this year … Rotten going to school in the afternoon.

12 Sunday
Went to Church in the morning. [By agreement with the Vicar of Stroud, our Headmaster, the Revd J. J. Walton ('Holy Joe') conducted a special service for the Brummagem flock, always exhorting its members to behave well. Attendances fluctuated – and behaviour? – difficult to assess.]

13 Monday
Borrowed Rigby's bike [school morning shift]. Went for a ride to Framilode in the afternoon with Syd, Choobe and Cox. Scrumped some apples. Had a parcel from Mom, pullover, vest.

Eric dressed in Sunday and 'High Days' best – a natty, three piece suit, note the waistcoat. In the buttonhole is the red poppy of Remembrance Day.

The parish church of Stroud.

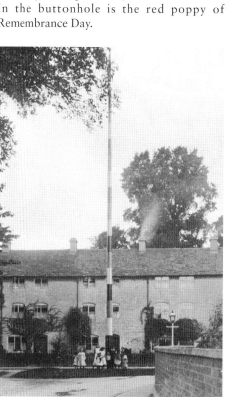

Although the postcard is over a century old, the maypole is older still. Paganhill.

14 Tuesday
Played football in the afternoon. Two first teams. We hope to play Stroud Central Secondary School soon. [Marling School had recently converted, for some bizarre reason, from the football to the rugby code.]

15 Wednesday
Went to the Gaumont at night with Syd and Mrs Wheatley. Quite a decent little cinema. [Rather a condescending tone, but the townie lad had, earlier in the year, taken Margaret to the Regal in Handsworth, a suburban cinema seating more than 2,000 patrons.] The Mikado. Very Good. Colouring, costume, acting and singing first class. Especially Koko.

16 Thursday
Syd and I throwing oranges at each other in the bedroom broke a vase. Mrs Wheatley annoyed. Quite rightly too.

Mrs Wheatley.

17 Friday

Atmosphere a little strained at breakfast but cleared up considerably at night. Picked up by Mrs Wheatley's sister next door in her car, with Mrs Wheatley. Went to Gloucester. Went in the 'Bon Marche'. Something like our Lewis's. Went again to the cathedral.

18 Saturday

Rain, rain, rain from a leaden sky. Had to receive an evacuee ... they rolled up in a car. Took them to Ebley and found kid's billet. Felt sorry for him. Bravely kept his tears back when he said goodbye to his father. [Life could be much tougher for youngsters than for lads in my own age group. Given my thirst for new experiences and new knowledge, I never felt homesick in Stroud. But I do confess to an occasional yearning for bacon and egg at home.]

Pals again!

19 Sunday
Beautiful morning. After Church went walk to Pitchcombe and Painswick. 8 miles before dinner.

20 Monday
Have to leave school at quarter past four now due to blackout and because of end of summer time. Go home from school in dark.

*

[With such long, dark evenings, a variety of games were brought into regular use: crib, solo whist, dominoes, bagatelle, chess, draughts. Let me digress. Sometimes, 'straitened circumstances' can develop the valuable by-product of improvisation. The photograph illustrates the point. 'Played chess' occurs frequently in the 1939 diary. Clearly the chess men have their tin box but the Wheatleys possessed no standard issue chess board. For my 'wizard wheeze' Mrs Wheatley allowed me to take an old pastry board and to chalk the appropriate squares on the board. A very stable base as can be seen. Other points of possible interest include Mrs Wheatley wearing the type of pinny to be seen throughout the land and me wearing a grey pullover, skilfully knitted by my mother with a black and yellow (school colours) edging around the neck. The short curl of hair on my forehead, known at the time as a kiss-curl, had but a short, uneventful life and later photographs will show that it has disappeared.]

Ebley, Stroud.

Pitchcombe.

Painswick.

Painswick Post Office.

Enjoying a game of chess with the Wheatleys.

Minchinhampton war memorial and church, just off the High Street.

*

21 Tuesday
Hope I get in team to play against Central.

22 Wednesday
Free morning ... borrowed Rigby's bike and cycled with Choobe and Syd to Minchinhampton. Super RAF aerodrome there, immense activity, camouflaged hangars. Super Havard training planes. [Syd was becoming clued up on aircraft recognition.]

23 Thursday
P. T. this morning. Skittle ball once more. Super game but covered with sweat as usual when I had finished. Vest soaking. [While I have quite forgotten the rules of skittle ball, the game was an ideal way for working off some of the vigorous, boisterous pep of the older boys.]

25 Saturday
Frank [the Wheatley's son] and his wife came again. Quite a little party. Bandwaggon again. A.1. Had a hot bath. Went to bed.

*

[There may be a tiny echo of Samuel Pepys about Saturday's entry – but not about Bandwagon. Even before war broke out 'Auntie Beeb' began to loosen her stays, acknowledging, in effect, that there was a lot to be said for having more light entertainment on the air. In 1938, Bandwagon, a variety show hit the airwaves, partly to combat the growing competition from commercial radio. The show's two regular stars were 'Big-Hearted' Arthur Askey and 'Stinker' Murdoch. The show quickly became very popular featuring odd-ball characters like Mrs Bagwash and daughter Nausea. One of the show's catch-phrases, widely used by the public, was, 'proper 'umdrum', which much of life can be unless leavened frequently with humour.]

*

26 Sunday
Went a walk with Choobe ... through Thrupp across muddy fields, Bisley Road. Dull, rainy and windy but I enjoyed the ramble very much. Marvellous view at one place. Severn could be seen for several miles along its length.

27 Monday
Had a letter from Margaret. Wants to know if I will see her. Will I? I should say so. Went to the Gaumont at night with Mrs W and S. Great dancing by G. R. and F. A. [Ginger Rogers and Fred Astaire in *The Story of Vernon and Irene Castle*.]

The Stars of *Bandwagon*.

Above: A view of the River Severn.

Right: Ginger Rogers and Fred Astaire.

"Mind Out, Mister, He's Got a Gun!" : *An Anxious Cinema Audience at a Children's Matinée*
The cinemagoer on the right is a connoisseur. He knows all about Westerns. He settles himself back in his chair like a blasé film critic. But the cinema-goer next to him is on tenterhooks. At any moment he may jump to his feet to warn the cowboy that the villain is creeping up on him from behind.

KIDS' MATINEE

Highlight of the week for thousands of evacuated children is the Saturday morning matinée at the local cinema.

TO-DAY, in the reception areas, the special Saturday morning cinema matinées for the children are fuller than ever. The evacuee children are mostly experienced cinema fans, and many authorities are glad to get them out of the way for an hour or so. The films which the exhibitors have been choosing especially for these Kids' Matinees suggest that the cartoon and the "Cowboy and Indian" types are most popular. Children ask for action and for laughs. "Felix the Cat" started it, "Oswald the Rabbit" looked like taking the laurels, until Mickey Mouse came along. Donald Duck with his almost incomprehensible squawk is now first favourite. They can sympathise with Donald Duck. His escapades are those of the naughty boy who will inevitably be punished. As such they can laugh at him with the unconscious cruelty of children waiting for the inevitable ending, be it being blown up by a bomb he is late in delivering, savaged by an eagle whose egg he is stealing, or at the mercy of the automatic robots for interfering with the museum exhibits.

Mickey Mouse, on the other hand, is the children's hero. You cannot laugh at your hero when he is in difficulties. And thousands wait breathlessly until his troubles are safely at an end. Mickey—unlike Donald —always gets a happy ending.

The Faces that Follow the Fortunes of Donald Duck
They are the most regular of all filmgoers. They seldom miss their own Saturday morning matinée. In reception areas these children's matinées are more popular than ever. And many authorities, who are all for keeping evacuees off the streets, bless the name of Mickey Mouse.

Efforts were made to keep us evacuees entertained!

29 Wednesday

Managed after great difficulty to borrow a bike. Went for a ride with Syd, Choobe and young Guise. [By now, even a casual reader just skimming through the book, will have spotted my frequent cadging for the loan of a bike. Any sensitivity or awkwardness I felt at these times was overwhelmed by the desire to enjoy the countryside. Pedal pushing would take me further and faster than 'Shank's Pony', although I did do a fair bit of tramping about. Here is another instance of my feeling at a material disadvantage, a feeling that hopefully did not become a fixation.]

30 Thursday

Well, Russia has started on Finland now ... still ploughing through Arnold's poems at night. [Matthew Arnold, noted Victorian poet.]

Chapter 4
December 1939

2 Saturday
Choobe came and we played solo, dominoes and crib. First class Bandwagon again.
[Choobe was in something of a fix, being billeted on his own with devout Baptists.
Maybe his hosts tried to convert him to their faith but whatever the reasons, this
quiet, slightly morose lad sought refuge in our gambling den at every opportunity.
Not that we ever played for stakes, but simply for good humoured amusement.]

3 Sunday
Church Parade this morning. About half the school there. Joe preached. Lousy,
bilgish. Sous le bras.* Went for a walk to Whiteshill with Choobe and Syd. Choobe
had to go to church again in the afternoon and so I borrowed his bike and went
with Syd to Minchinhampton to watch RAF trainers at work ... Grand coming
down Cowcombe Hill. [*Under the arm – at the time an expression denoting
great scorn and contempt. The hill referred to was long, steep, with tricky bends
providing exhilaration sufficient to blast away the residue of a duff sermon. Even
with all this attractive and interesting sight-seeing, I was revising hard for the
approaching end of term exams. I didn't want to let my parents down and if either
Mom or Dad wished to voice a triumphal 'I told you so', I hoped it would be Mom
on the basis of good results. Revision continued but...]

4 Monday
Stopped in and did some English revision except for a few intervals when I played
chess and draughts & dominoes with Choobe and Syd. [The intellectual equivalents
to slices of lemon at half-time in a rugged football match?]

5 Tuesday
We had a little snow.

7 Thursday
Court asked four of us to take table down to Co-op Hall because they haven't
enough room to seat all boys. What a lark. Dashing through Cainscross on a dull
December afternoon with a table. Great fun. [An operation not unlike requiring
condemned men to build the gallows to be used on the morrow. I was rather given
to flights of fancy, probably still am, the legacy left from reading the working class
equivalents of 'ripping yarns' e.g. Rockfist Rogan and Wolf of Kabul found in boys'

'Choobe', the long suffering lad.

Rack Hill, viewed from Cowcombe Hill, Chalford.

papers like Adventure and The Wizard. Mr A. N. Court was a new member of staff to teach French. Young, dapper, enthusiastic, it was much easier to associate with him than with some of the middle aged, more distant in attitude, teachers.]

8 Friday
Exams ... Had to walk to Cainscross in the driving rain. What a place to take exams. Boards on trestles. Rocking like mad when anyone moved. English not too bad. Got absolutely soaked coming back even though I was partly under an umbrella with Lowe and Archer.

9 Saturday
...Prose into French perfectly chronic, [Code for very difficult] Choobe, Syd and I went to the Gaumont. Gracie Fields picture* better than expected ... forgot to fill boiler for Syd's bath. [Syd very seldom lost his rag – can't remember whether he did on this occasion. He had due cause. *Shipyard Sally* – boosting the war effort.]

10 Sunday
No compulsory Church parade ... didn't get up till half-past nine. Walked [with Syd and Choobe] up Butterow Hill to Rodborough Common. Plenty of flying. We had two pairs of field glasses and we made very interesting studies of the aeroplanes. Choobe had to go to church in the afternoon. Poor kid. Don't know how he sticks it where he is. I couldn't or wouldn't.

6-12-39.

Dear Mother,

Thanks very much for your letter. Another one to add to my ever increasing pile of souvenirs. Except for a slight cold, nothing to be worried about, I am still in the best of spirits and health. I hope you are contented and as well as am.

The books from Cornishe's arrived this morning, so I am now completely fitted out with all the necessary articles that I require. The exams are very close now, and I am swotting like mad to try an obtain a good result. I shall of course do my best but I doubt if the results will be too good. The masters will out of necessity be forced to set easier papers than ofusual.

Not much ~~holiday~~ is it, ten days? The masters have been complaining but the Head is adamant in his decision. As far as I know there is no-one who is not returning home at Christmas. There are very few signs of any festive spirit down here. I shall

A letter to Mother.

be wanting some extra money soon please, if you can afford to spare it, in order to buy some Christmas presents. You can send that money which has been given to me.

Yesterday morning we had snow, and then it cleared up to be a beautiful afternoon, just when we had to go to school. I shall have several photographs to show you when I get home. Syd. took them and developed them and they have turned out quite well.

Had one of Dad's hilgish, sloppy philosophical discourses this morning. Proper Senneca isn't he? Leastways he thinks he is. Glad to hear that Jack has had a fortnight's leave. He must have had some wonderful experiences. Tell Dad I will write to him soon but I shall not have much time to write letters for week or so. Thank him for me very much for the postal-order. I will certainly write to Uncle Walter when I find time.

Well so long a bit,

Lots of love from,

Your affectionate son,

Eric,

This popular song from the 1920s struck a particular chord during the war years, the second line of the lyric being something like, 'when we must say goodbye'.

My wartime home town, Stroud.

17 Sunday
Graf Spee's time limit expires at 9.30 pm today. 7 Allied warships waiting for her outside river Plate. Bitterly cold. Cox fainted right across me in Church and Reeves and I had to carry him out. Poor kid. Dragged Syd out in the afternoon and we went for a most enjoyable walk. Fourty acres. Bisley Road. Beautiful feeling of joie de vivre.

18 Monday
Graf Spee scuttled herself in entrance to Montevideo harbour. Hitler's orders.
[A victory for the Allies but of an unusual kind. The *Graf Spee* was a pocket battleship much prized by the Germans and potentially a great hazard to our merchant shipping. This success constituted a great boost to morale, demonstrating that German might was not invincible. A film was made of what happened.]

19 Tuesday
Got to play chess tomorrow against Marling. [One of the very few times that the schools fraternised.]

*

[Of course, there was more to life in Stroud than playing chess, enjoying hot baths and larking about generally. Six days a week I trudged to school and back, sometimes more than once a day when organised games were on the agenda. Our snug billet was literally but a stone's throw from Stroud's town centre and I would

Butter Row, Stroud.

Admiral Graf Spee.

HMS *Ajax*. One of the British cruisers that had harried the *Graf Spee*.

set off for school along picturesque Church Street and then drop down along High Street or George Street, sometimes along King Street, to reach the start of Cainscross Road. Unlike the winding hill charm of the town centre with its numerous pleasant small shops, Cainscross Road was relatively humdrum, not dissimilar from some of the flattish suburban roads of Birmingham. The return walk (Syd, of course, cycled) from Marling School might well include nipping along Lansdown Road and cutting through the churchyard back into Church Street.]

*

20 *Wednesday*

Poona [Mr Thomas, Deputy Headmaster] reckons I ought to go to university. Hope I can. It would be great. Stayed on after school had broken up. Won my game of chess. Hot dog. Winning 3-2 when I left. Frank and Amy came down. Gave us luminous plaques. Specially made in lab. Mrs W gave me a pair of socks. [A kind and caring family, the Wheatleys. The plaques-discs about an inch in diameter that became luminous in the dark. They may potentially have been intended as an aid in the blackout. I have no further knowledge of them.]

21 *Thursday*

What a difference to be seen between Brum and Stroud. Ugh! Nauseating.

Church Street, Stroud.

High Street, Stroud.

High Street, Stroud.

Lansdown Road, Stroud.

A seasonal postcard from Stroud.

Work-a-day Birmingham.

[A little ambiguous perhaps but I had temporarily forgotten that Birmingham was an industrial city, its homes and factories fuelled by coal. Even so, things were bucking up at home in the way of material comforts. War can bring jobs, better incomes and improved pocket money.]

22 Friday
Difference becomes more marked every day. Feel a kind of repulsion for city life now. Give me the wide open spaces.

25 Monday
Had a card off Frank and Amy this morning. Beautiful morning. Sun shining. But what a difference between a fine day in Brum and a fine day in Stroud.
[The Christmas interlude was very enjoyable, visiting relatives, renewing old friendships with Evan and Eddie who were now in paid employment.]

30 Saturday
Saw Margaret. First time for over five months. Dressed very well. Looked radiant ... makes me want to like her more. [Clearly, there was some hesitancy on my part. Even to a diary, I was not then prepared to use another and stronger four letter word beginning with 'l'].

Chapter 5

January 1940

1 Monday

Saw Margaret in the afternoon. She looked grand. Went to the Villa Cross [cinema]. Wouldn't let me hold her hand. Kept her gloves on. Wonder why. O.K. afterwards though for she allowed me to kiss her goodbye. "Oh a kiss long as my exile ..., and my true lip hath virgin'd it e'er since." [Shakespeare, *Coriolanus*, one of our set books.]

3 Wednesday

There were never four hundred boys on the train. Arrived in Stroud about half past twelve. Mr Wheatley very bad. Seems to be touch and go. We will try to help Mrs Wheatley as much as we can. Hope we don't have to leave School House. Borrowed a toboggan. Hurtled down slopes of Rodborough. Went to pictures in evening. Palatial modern cinema. Thought we might have to sleep in armchairs. Settled down to do so. [Mr Wheatley had spent much of his life at sea, in the merchant navy I believe, and suffered from chest troubles, including long bouts of violent coughing.]

4 Thursday

Started back ... terribly cold in school especially in library. Did some work, both home and house. The Wheatleys are going to leave School House for good. We might be able to go with them.

5 Friday

Free afternoon today. Choobe, Syd and I climbed up Selsley Hill. Really marvellous view of surrounding countryside. Much better than from Rodborough. Not very clear but Marling School could be seen. Syd made the cup chocolate. Not a bad effort. Mrs Wheatley was with Mr W who was having an attack.

6 Saturday

What a job it is washing up. Still this will be an experience to look back on in years to come. Four masters going back to Brum at G. Dixons. Poon, Froggy, Gogs, & Allison. [Those masters taught History, French, Science and Maths. George Dixons School in City Road was open for its own boys and the increasing number of HGS boys who were remaining at home.]

Right: Basil Rathbone, Star of *The Sun Never Sets*, New Years Day 1940.

Below: A souvenir postcard announcing, 'The First Anniversary of this increasingly Popular Picture House Monday, May 22nd 1916.'

A lovely view of Rodborough Fort.

The view transformed in a charming watercolour by the well-known postcard artist A. R. Quinton.

The view from Selsley, near Stroud.

Bulls Cross, near Painswick.

7 Sunday
Mr Wheatley seems easier today. Hooray. Beautiful morning. Went for a long walk after Church. Old Painswick Road, Bulls Cross. Delightful country. Grand, exhilarating. Went another long walk in aft. 40 acres. Syd could hardly walk back. Fun. Stoked fires.

8 Monday
Mr Wheatley nearly out of the wood now. Thank God! Beautiful day but couldn't go out because someone had to stay in the house with Mr Wheatley. Improving in my French proses. Now that I give mine in last I get a much better and fairer comment. [Timing can be so important in life!]

9 Tuesday
Seem to have been here months now instead of a week. Amy came to tea. Had some usual witty backchat with her. Great fun. A more cheerful atmosphere seems predominant in the house now. Choobe, Syd and I went to the Ritz in the evening. I thoroughly enjoyed *Goodbye, Mr Chips*. Excellent acting by Robert Donat. [Amy, a young wife, pretty and ready to tease the bashful, embarrassed Syd about his attractive locks and the target he would be for young ladies who had anything about them.]

10 Wednesday
Wonder how true these reports about the Finns annihilating Russians by the thousands are. Don't tell you how many they lose. What a racket. Very cold but sunny today. Fetched my overcoat from the cleaners. They have made quite a good job of it. Think how grand it would be if I could spend one of these beautiful evenings with Margaret, walking together under the starry vault. [From the poetic to the prosaic.]

11 Thursday
Amy came and helped to cook the dinner. Syd developed some of his photos later so I finished off Hamlet. Stoked up the fires again.

12 Friday
Stoked the fires and had some fun in a wheelbarrow. Choobe leaving Shipways tomorrow. Made Syd laugh by making up rhymes in songs about the girl at Peckhams. Pull his leg blind but he takes it all in good part. [Peckhams – a shop that sourced some of Syd's photographic requirements. Whether he had designs of a romantic nature I never found out, but I think Amy was on the right track.]

13 Saturday
By all accounts Choobe has a splendid billet.

14 Sunday
Another sharp frost. Walked to Choobe's new billet & then round King's Court. Lovely view, lovely day. Life worth living. "I love man not the less but nature more."

Robert Donat

Left: A favourite British actor, Robert Donat.

Below: A scene from the film *Goodbye, Mr Chips*. This greatly popular teacher was played by Robert Donat. In retirement, he invites senior schoolboys to tea. The lads ask, 'How long will it last sir?' meaning the First World War, a question that persisted through the Second World War.

Fountain Street, Nailsworth.

Nailsworth.

Walked to Nailsworth in the aft. Quaint straggling village. Wrote English essay evening. Stoked fires. [To keep adjoining school warm.]

15 Monday
Very nice letter [from Margaret] She uses June perfume ... wants me to buy her some ... we'll see, we'll see. [My cagey reaction would have nothing to do with shortage of ardour but shortage of funds.] Stoking fires a regular nightly ritual now. Quite enjoyable and certainly a novel experience.

16 Tuesday
Froze hard during night. Turned up late for organised walk, followed the crowd a little way, then turned off and went along canal, or to be more exact, a backwater. Frozen several inches thick. Slid about a bit ... cause Syd fell down. Three of our boys can skate quite well. Had to stay in because of not turning up for walk. In the evening, as it was so fine and clear went running to Star Inn, up Slad Road and back. Great running along, frosty, snowy roads in moonlight. Syd on his bike paced me. Feel very fit now.

17 Wednesday
Choobe, Syd and I were taken over the 'Erinoid' factory by Frank. Extremely interesting. Took us the whole way through, from raw material kasene [casein?] to finished Erinoid substance. Astonishing variety of smells. Some pleasant but mostly unpleasant. Deafening clatter in most parts, awful atmosphere and tedious routine. Mechanical like motions of workers. It would never suit me to work in a factory. Dust, fumes, grime, dirt; pulsating, throbbing, clattering machinery. Sweat. Ugh! What a life. A morning very well spent. Stoked fires. [Probably an unusual experience for evacuees. The mode of expression was perhaps a bit over the top. But then I was still an apprentice.]

18 Thursday
Johnnie going to a Social & Dance in the evening. Gave him some hints (me of all people) on dancing. He was seething with excitement. His first romance ... went to the Ritz in the evening with Syd and Choobe. No one to touch Bing for crooning. [At the back of this diary is a list of films seen in the year including East Side of Heaven, co-star Joan Blondell. Film evaluated as 'Pleasing entertainment for blackout blues.']

19 Friday
Woke up to find snow on the ground. Countryside looks very beautiful under its mantle of white. Johnnie got on O.K. at the dance. He's in heaven. Makes me feel like home. Snow-balled with Syd coming home. Great fun. Threw snowballs into Holloways. Open door of Engine Room. One went right in. No one came out. Plastered the front of the house with snowballs. [Holloway Brothers were one of Stroud's major employers, a clothing factory situated in Brick Row.]

Above: Thought to be on the Painswick Road.

Right: Crooner Bing Crosby.

Bing Crosby

JOAN BLONDELL

Left: Joan Blondell, Star of *East Side of Heaven.*

Below: Thought to be Grange Fields.

Syd, being a developing photographer in a double sense, made mistakes but this may have been a deliberate lark.

20 *Saturday*

Snow froze during the night. Went on the ice afterwards. Slid for a bit. Fun. Lindley and his two nips there sliding. [A youngish teacher of German]. Had a discussion with Court in the afternoon. No one knew what he was talking about. Seems to be a big pot at concerts at Ritz. Decent chap but thinks quite a bit of himself.

21 *Sunday*

Scouts Church Service this morning. Some nasty cracks in sermon about rowdiness of our school. Went a long walk in the afternoon. Syd took snap of me on car. Along old Painswick Road and back along new. Beautiful snowy scenery. Wonder why I have not heard from home.

22 *Monday*

Heard nothing from home for a week now. Probably pipes are frozen and they are having some difficulty in obtaining water. Just popped along to Church Institute to see how Recreation Club was getting along. Quite a number there. New idea of Joe's. Good one for once. Every morning, chess, games T. T. etc. Hot milk for boys who have free morning. Obtained permission off Baggy* to miss shower and walk tomorrow and to go and see meeting of hounds at Quedgeley. Contemplate going to boxing matches at Liberal Hall next Monday. [*Nickname of senior French teacher, Mr Lindon (see also p 153)].

23 Tuesday

At last a letter from Mom. Every one O.K. thank goodness. Set off early for Quedgeley. Choobe came so borrowed Worrall's bike. Grand riding along snowy roads. Found to our disappointment that there was no meeting. Most likely cancelled owing to state of ground. Rode to the Severn, which was frozen. Larked about on the ice. Tested it at edge. 8ft stick went right through but didn't reach river bed. Wouldn't stand much chance if any one fell in there. Syd took a snap of me on ice, also one of me in a wheelbarrow, with Choobe pushing it, under a signpost pointing to the Bristol Road. A most enjoyable morning. Went to the Ritz in the evening and saw *Beau Geste* and *Arrest Bulldog Drummond* twice through. [On and off screen a day of stirring adventure. Gary Cooper and Ray Milland starred in *Beau Geste*, Reginald Denny appeared in *Bulldog Drummond* and Eric Armstrong did a solo turn in Follies on Ice.]

24 Wednesday

Lot warmer today. Thawing. Have certainly got a cold. Wonder where from. [I doubt if I made a connection with the 'follies'!] Don't feel like going out. Had a letter from Dad. Mr Wheatley hopes to get up tomorrow evening. Can do so if he has a good night's sleep. Stoked fires.

25 Thursday

Don't feel so good today but alright in spirits. Poor old Syd doesn't seem too good. Sits over fire all time. Popped in Institute ... seems quite a good scheme. Plenty of boys there playing games and generally enjoying themselves. Mr Wheatley got up today. First time for five weeks. Pretty weak on his pins. Syd went to bed after tea. Seems to have caught an influenza cold. Wrote a letter to Dad. Stoked fires with Mrs Wheatley. [Yes, diary entries can be so easily misinterpreted!]

26 Friday

Syd staying in bed today. Raining like mad. Wish Syd was better. Three P.S,'s. [Periods at school set aside for private study]. Had a chalk fight with Johnnie. [Sticks of chalk broken into pieces and used as missiles, just a distraction from hard study.] ... Johnnie seems a little under the weather. Helped Mrs Wheatley stoke the fires. Read some *Capitaine Fracasse* and finished *La mare au diable*. Made Syd laugh a little.

27 Saturday

Rained like mad, so didn't go to P.T. Went and fetched the dinner, and got my own. Took the umbrella in the afternoon to school. Joe gave us a lecture about behaviour in Church tomorrow. What a rotten Saturday evening I spent. Looked at Picture Posts and did some sketching. Syd seems pretty bad to-night. Did fires and had a bath.

PICTURE

POST

BOR 72

"YOUNG BILL" GOES OFF

The *Picture Post*, popular during the war years.

28 Sunday

Hooray! Syd a lot better this morning. Choobe called and we went to Church. Only about 100 boys there. Slippy as glass underfoot. Syd got up s'arternoon. Played crib with Mr Wheatley in evening. Hope I hear from Margaret tomorrow.

29 Monday

Three letters... [But not one from Margaret]. Been snowing for 48 hrs in Brum. Snow on the ground here. What weather. Worst for years. Trains held up all over the country. General dislocation. Went to the Boxing Tournament in the evening. [Held in the Liberal Hall]. Not many there, but enjoyed myself immensely. Several good scraps. Three knock-outs. One chap went through ropes. What a tough crowd watch boxing matches. Interesting survey of human nature could be made from their faces. All characters. [What prompted this excursion into the unknown, I can't recall. We were not a pugilistic family. Simply schoolboy curiosity? There has been no second round.]

25-1-40.

Dear Dad,

Many thanks for letter containing a mine of philosophical wealth, and also material wealth which is far more useful. Now I can go to a big Boxing Tournament which is to be held in the Liberal Hall next Monday evening. It should be good and I am looking forward to it very much.

I am glad to be able to say that Mr Wheatley got up to day. The first time in five weeks. He went to bed early this evening. He seems to have caught the flu. I have got a cold myself but feel alright in spirits which is more important. Well at last the weather has taken a turn for the better.

"As in winter when the frost breaks up
....
Through all the world a dripping sound is heard"
You'll have to look to your poetic laurels if I continue in these vein.

You can tell Mom that I received the vests and trunks this morning. Please thank her very much. Gld to hear that Jacks and Les are o.k and that Sam & Bryan

Letter to Dad.

...e on the road to recovery. I am writing this letter while listening to 'Under the Shadow of the Swastika'. I hope you are listening to it. I see they are making a serial of it in "Reynolds News". Are you going in for the competition for picking a War Time Cabinet of your own? You should do well.

We rode to the Severn on Tuesday morning. I was almost able to get to the other side, the ice was so thick. We had hoped to see a meeting of the Berkley hounds but the meeting had been cancelled due to the condition of the ground. In the evening we went to see 'Beau Geste'. Quite a good picture.

Well I hope you will excuse this short letter but I am rather tired after doing homework, and want to go to bed early. Hoping you and Mum are quite well. Remember me to all.

Well, so long a bit.
Best wishes,
From your loving son,
Eric.

Poor weather never deterred larking about. Long suffering Choobe still seems to wear the tight lipped smile of the martyr.

A clip from 'Follies on Ice.'

Ray Milland.   Gary Cooper.

30 Tuesday

No letter from Margaret yet. [During the next few days some of the diary entries expressed, in rather unkind terms, my peevish impatience, so least said soonest mended.]

31 Wednesday

Mr Wheatley has got a cold. Hope he hasn't caught it off me. Joe wants Johnnie to go into the Ministry. Can't imagine Johnnie with a dog collar. Said himself to Joe that the spirit had not moved him yet. Played crib with Mr Wheatley. More like old times. Very slippy underfoot when going with Mrs Wheatley to see to the fires. [Syd was not yet up to snuff.]

Chapter 6
February 1940

1 Thursday
Letter from Dad. Seems that they are in a worse plight in Birmingham than we are in Stroud. No bread delivery. Hooray, at last a letter from Margaret. Apologises for being late in replying. Taking up cycling so she might pop down and see me. Would be O.K. if we could arrange a meeting place between here and Worcester. What a girl! Snowed this morning. Syd started school this afternoon.

2 Friday
Mr Wheatley does not seem to improve much. Went to the Gaumont. Crazy Gang extremely funny. Absolutely mad but make you laugh. Stoked fires when we came from pictures.

3 Saturday
Nothing very exciting happened at school. Joe kept us for another assembly. Larked about in schoolyard. Hoisted Syd's cap to the top of the flag-pole. [Next to School House, our billet.] Played crib with Mr Wheatley. Stoked fires then had a glorious hot bath. Cold gone now. Hooray!

4 Sunday
Thaw set in. Raining. Went a walk along London Road with Choobe after Church. Back through Thrupp. Wrote to Margaret. Proposed meeting her at half term. Be a row if I don't hear from her before Thurs. [Stupid boy!]

5 Monday
Mr Wheatley suffered a relapse. Crikey we are back from where we started. Mrs Wheatley seems worried to death. On the verge of tears all the while. Still we must set our teeth and grin and bear it. Thaw has certainly been quick. Had a letter from Mom and a Postal Order. No coal along at the end fire so we took some round in the barrow. Syd written home for flash powder so it should arrive soon. [The powder was not for boiler or explosive work but for flash photography! Syd was a keen amateur photographer.]

6 Tuesday
Joe told us this afternoon that there will be no half term but we shall have a long holiday at home at Easter, like we had at Christmas. What a swizz. Shall have to

take a day off if Margaret can see me. Joe will probably give me permission. All the same if he doesn't. [I could be stroppy if the cause was just!] Joe gave us some notes on Old Testament. Know little or nothing more about it now. He went so fast.

7 Wednesday
Mr Wheatley seems no better. Poor old Mrs Wheatley. Just when she should be living in comfortable retirement she has to work her fingers to the bone. In the evening Syd took a photo of me, with his newly arrived flash powder, while I was stoking the boiler. Should be a good photograph. [Sadly, no success.] On tenterhooks. Agony of suspense. Hope I hear from Margaret tomorrow.

8 Thursday
Crept half afraid downstairs this morning. Saw to my greatest delight that there was a letter from Margaret. Cannot go Saturday, hockey match. Sunday, cousin home on leave, but she can see me any Saturday or Sunday afterwards. Yippee! Added a P.S. that she didn't know whether I knew it, but she likes me very much. Je suis aux anges. Shall have to send her a Valentine now.

9 Friday
Slack day today. Rather a dull life. Bought a Valentine for Margaret. I am a funny kid. How my moods change. "The ways of man are manifold." [Source forgotten but worth a thought or two].

10 Saturday
Went to P.T. in the morning. Got back and found that Mr Wheatley was much worse. Touch and go again. Much worse than last time. Doctor and nurse been. Not much hope there appears. Mrs Wheatley broke down. Wonder how she has borne up so long. Frank and Amy are staying the night. We shall have to leave our billet. Great pity for we were very comfortable and happy here.

11 Sunday
Mr Wheatley still struggling on. Went a walk round fourty acres with Choobe and Syd. Frost has caused colossal damage to trees. Wonder where our new billet will be.

12 Monday
Went to the Billeting Office. Saw Mrs Angel. We are to call in again Wednesday morning, when we shall be told where to go and on Friday we shall move. Finished reading *Capitaine Fracasse* in P.S. [Private Study] Jolly good yarn. Best French Set Book we have to read.

13 Tuesday
Mr Wheatly still improving but he says the funniest wildest things. Light-headed, but he seems to have turned the corner. Went to football in the morning. The ground was as hard as iron, ball bouncing everywhere except the right place. It seems that

Locations awaiting schoolboy discovery – above Painswick.

Bisley.

Birdlip.

there will be a half term holiday after all. Joe's devout avowals to the contrary. Parents have complained, and so have masters, forcing his hand. Gosh have I got a sore throat. Hurts me to swallow. Fervently hope that I and the weather are O.K. for the twenty-fifth of this month.

14 Wednesday
Have almost lost my voice. Curse (in a croak). Sat in front of the fire reading. Acted as a patient for Frank who has to take his first aid test tomorrow. Bandaged me up all over the place. Shall have to start packing tomorrow.

15 Thursday
Had a letter off Margaret but no Valentine. Still, she said she was thrilled to bits. Sweetest thing I could have done. She can see me in a fortnight's time. No longer 'dear Eric' but 'dearest'. Yippee! Again je suis aux anges except that we have got to move tomorrow.

16 Friday
Well we moved in to our new billet. Took us two journeys to transport all our things. Mrs Robertson did not seem too friendly, but I think she was a little ill at ease. The Captain was a 'little seedy'. Saw him though. Proper army captain. 'Bai Jovian' accent. Red face. Probably fond of his whisky. Beautiful study. Real class. Our bedroom quite nice. Didn't see anywhere else. Pity Syd by himself here over the weekend. Snowing when we arrived at New Street. Atrocious weather. Snow in large mounds down either side of the roads. Good to see Mom and Dad again. Wonder how Sydney's getting on.

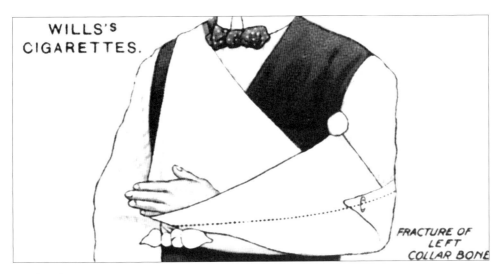

Bandaged up!

*

[17 Saturday–18 Sunday was for me the evacuee's equivalent of the serviceman's 48 hour pass and was pleasant enough, as I moved contentedly through the overlapping circles of family and friends. Although the war remained relatively quiet, it had not disappeared from the radar of experience. We were now in the period of what came to be known as the 'phoney war'. Although fully accurate figures were not disclosed, our merchant shipping losses were worryingly high. The rationing of butter, sugar and bacon had begun. The iciest winter for many years had delayed, for instance, new military attacks by the Russians against the Finns. And the fact that no serious air attacks had yet been made on Britain affected the numbers of evacuees. Figures show that of the about three quarters of a million unaccompanied children who had left home on 1 September 1939, over 300,000 had returned home. At our home, one particular attack by Jack Frost had not been allowed for.]

*

19 *Monday*
Lavatory pipe burst. Water cascading down the wall. Had to knock the pipe up. Quite fun. Well I wonder how I shall get on tomorrow at Stafford House.

20 *Tuesday*
Water gushing forth from burst pipe this morning. [So much for brute force!] Mom saw me off at station. Played Newmarket on the way down. Dinner ready when I got in. Beautiful dining room. Lace mats, serviettes. Silver plate everywhere. Huge sideboards. Everything bright and lustrous. This certainly is a high class billet, and they certainly don't starve. Don't see much of the Captain. Breakfast not until ten o'clock! Hot brick wrapped in flannel and placed in bed at night. Captain drinks whisky like

Muriel Richards, still wearing her evacuee label.

Strength in and by numbers, evacuees in the grounds of the Bishop's Palace, Chichester. Three hundred children were billeted at the palace.

water and smokes cigarettes by the dozen. If the friendly easy going atmosphere of the Wheatleys is missing, we are more fortunate in other respects. More amenities. Had a lovely hot bath in the evening.

21 *Wednesday*

Did some homework in bed but did not get up until nine o'clock. Certainly is a pleasant change to wash in a decent bathroom. Had a splendid breakfast. Mrs Robertson is a grand cook. Did a little work on the Communist Manifesto, then went a short walk. Stream at the bottom of garden. Another stream, canal, and railway only a few yards away, and plenty of fields and dales to roam in. Spent a very pleasant half-hour exploring. Beautiful garden here. Cap spends his time in it, wheeling barrow loads of 'muck' about. 26 fowl, orchard, and well laid out flower beds. [Did any of this portend what my career might be? A smallholder, an over particular accountant, a youthful commissar?]

22 *Thursday*

Nothing happened at school. Finished Karl Marx in the evening. Hooray! Went for a little walk in the moonlight after supper. Really beautiful. Stood on bridge and watched clouds pass over moon, and the moonlight glittering in the water. Houses nestling on bosom of hill in fitful moonlight looked really breathtaking. Lovely warm breeze. Not long until Sunday now.

23 *Friday*

Went to Mrs Wheatley's and took back the case which she lent me to take home. Mr Wheatley got up for a little while yesterday. Had a pleasant chat with him. Did

Stroud, away to the left.

The hamlet of Amberley, near Stroud.

some crosswords in the evening. What should be the brightest and liveliest part of the day is the dullest. Had a bath, which goes part of the way to make up for a dull evening. *War Illustrated*, and *Illustrated* are a real boon and blessing. Wrote a short letter to Margaret to remind her of our date.

24 *Saturday*
Went to Wheatleys, borrowed a thermos for the great adventure tomorrow. Had my hair cut. Less weight to carry. Bought some pop and chocolates in order to eke our supplies tomorrow. Shall have to get up at six, so went to bed at nine o'clock. Yippee!

25 *Sunday*
Dark when started. Lovely riding through the dawn. Little traffic. Severn Stoke pretty little place. Margaret late as usual but she looked grand. Improving if it's possible as she grows older. Sweet girl. Went for a short ride left our bikes at a farmstead. Walked. Lovely. Margaret quiet but she has a cold. Still good to see her again. Hope to see her at Easter. Did 70 miles today. Nearly done. Bath welcome. [Now and again, I did wonder whether our days of heady romance of just a year ago, would ever return.]

26 *Monday*
We are playing the Shell tomorrow. Hope we can wipe out our defeat and vindicate our honour.

War Illustrated.

Eric ready for the off – on someone else's steed!

27 Tuesday
Raining ... it seemed doubtful whether we should play. It was eventually decided that we could. Pitch extremely muddy. Very tiring. But just the game and conditions I like. We won 4-1. And I scored two goals! First time I have scored for months and months, probably years. Rumour that we shall play the Central on Saturday, and that I shall be captain. Hope so! Had interesting conversation with Cap at night.

28 Wednesday
Speech Day ... left School about quarter past four. Beautiful afternoon ... we called for Choobe and went for a walk.

29 Thursday
Lovely morning. Beautiful blue sky, warm sun and not a trace of cloud. Baggy showed me the letter he received from Stroud Central School. They are quite willing to play us on Saturday morning on their field. I am to be captain. Picked team with help of Round, Tookey & Ralls. Think we ought to win. Went a walk with Choobe and Syd. Could see the Severn quite distinctly from Rodborough. [The walking season was getting into its stride again.]

Chapter 7
March 1940

1 Friday

Gosh it is going to be awful trying to work these beautiful light nights. [Probably double summer time was in operation.] Mrs Robertson told us today that we should have to leave as her health was being impaired and that she could not stand the strain of extra work. What a lot of tommy rot. They never wanted us in the first place, so why not be honest about the whole thing. What a difference from Mrs Wheatley.

2 Saturday

Match against Central gave a different result to what I expected. We lost 1-2. But nobody to blame. Our forwards could not finish off their good work and we were hesitating in front of goal. However it was a rattling good game and I enjoyed it very much. We hope to play them again if possible. Rotten at school this afternoon. [Saturday remember.]

3 Sunday

Went a walk in the morning to Minchinhampton. Really delightful on top of common breathing the clean fresh air. Messed about till four then walked to Brimscombe along the canal. Very pleasant evening.

4 Monday

Baggy told us this afternoon where our new billet is. It is North something or other in the 'Uplands'. There will be about twelve of us in a big house and the numbers will be gradually increased to about fifty. Baggy and his wife are living there too. Should be very nice. Just like a boarding school. Hope the kids who will also be there are O.K. Hope we can get some work done.

5 Tuesday

Played football ... a pretty poor sort of game ... everyone messing and larking about on an inferior pitch. Went to a Lloyds Table Tennis Club afterwards with Tookey, Brakewell, Williams and Merriman. Had a few games, but it is a pretty poor sort of dump. Had to suffer Joe reading and discussing Rabbi-Ben Arra this afternoon. It simply is waste of a lesson, having to sit back and listen to him yob. Pretty poor i'faith. Well we shall soon be gone from the Robertsons, but Mrs Robertson seems to be trying to make amends by making it as comfortable as possible for us.

Swells Hill, Brimscombe, near Stroud.

Brimscombe, Stroud Valley.

Brimscombe Station.

Still I expect she will be very glad to see the back of us. [Over the years I have occasionally wondered whether there were reasons additional to that of 'too much work for the memsahib', for our dismissal from a cushy 'posting'. Perhaps the captain did not see us as potential officer material – more like Bolshie Brummies given The Communist Manifesto that had been left lying around.]

6 Wednesday
Lovely day again and it certainly seems that Spring is on the way. Hooray. Two weeks from today we shall be home but we don't know how long for. It is rumoured that we may have three weeks. Hope so.

7 Thursday
It's going to be a job lugging suit-cases up to Uplands.

8 Friday
Well we moved in the afternoon. What a cussed, diabolical, sweaty job. Great big house. Still wants a lot of doing up. There are 14 of us here at present, Syd and I, Coe, Shaw, Karsey, Kent, Griffith, Heath, Davenport, Potter, Quance, Millichip, Forster, Madeley. Not too bad a lot. Hope no more than this come. Went round garden in evening. Lot of digging to be done. There are two greenhouses, conservatory, common room, tennis court. Just like a boarding school. Mrs Lindon very helpful. Should be O.K. here. Table tennis table to be fixed up. Scope in dining room.

This old postcard is franked 1910. A tower and steeple were added to the church during the 1930s.

A front view of Northfield, Folly Lane.

A view of Northfield from the tennis court.

One of several groups of 'Northfieldites'. Snake buckle belts are still in vogue for boys in short trousers. (Photographer H. L. Sharpley, i.e. Syd)

9 Saturday
Bit of a pull having to get up at quarter past seven. French exam this morning. Not too bad. Spent a pleasant afternoon in the garden lazing away the time. Had table-tennis tournaments in the evening. Decent kids Len Shaw, Stan Coe & Karsey.

10 Sunday
Went to Church this morning. Not many boys there. Called in at Ma Wheatleys. She gave me ten shillings which she maintains she owes Mom. Had some fun with 'Chips'. He's hanging round Phyllis the maid. [The government paid allowances to very many parents of evacuees and the money was passed to the 'foster' parents.]

11 Monday
Sat in the garden in the evening and swotted French literature, though attention somewhat distracted by the activities of 'Chips' and 'Hitler' who were doing their best to annihilate one another by throwing canes at each other. What a life.

12 Tuesday
French literature this morning. Not too bad. Think I have done O.K. in all exams so far ... we have quite good food, if not quite enough of it. Madely brought his portable wireless set. Quite good. Played table tennis and narrowly avoided defeat.

13 Wednesday
Last exam tomorrow. Wish Coe and Shaw were not going tomorrow. [Back to their old billet]. Everyone preparing a hot welcome for fatty B if he turns up. He seems to be extremely unpopular.

*

[To a limited extent Northfield served as an evacuees' transit camp coping with arrivals and departures, the billeting situation always changing. Syd and I being senior boys and among the first of the projected fifty, assumed the status of 'Old Sweats'. We were each 'in charge' of a dormitory of high spirited lads. Among these was Dennis, younger brother of Margaret, a rebellious youngster who had walked out of his billet. He was a welcome recruit, opening up new lines of possible communication, 'a link with Worcester' where his family were staying.]

*

14 Thursday
Ah well, exams are all over now, I can enjoy my leisure time with ease. Played table tennis this afternoon and went a walk up Slad Road, through woods, and back down Folly Lane.

15 Friday
Walked to Robertsons. Letter from Margaret there. She makes no mention about arrangements for holidays. What a Scatterbrain she is. Mrs Robertson informed me that Dad had written 'Capt' a "very offensive letter". Expect it was about allowance for my keep. Eleven Northfieldites went to the Gaumont in the evening. Great fun trooping through Stroud. 'Eleven sixes please'. Called in a fish and chip shop on the way back. Great life this. Such fun. Real 'esprit de corps' exists in the building. [The film was *The Rains Came* starring Myrna Loy and Tyrone Power. My appraisal, at the end of this diary includes, 'little too many clinches'. Of course, by clinch I meant warm embrace of the romantic kind. I was starved and envious.]

16 Saturday
Walked to Choobe's this morning to borrow his bike for tomorrow as we are going to Cirencester. He is still officially in quarantine. Rather unfortunate for him. Must have felt lonely in this state of enforced idleness. [A case of mumps I believe.] New fags not too bad and Weedon O.K.

17 Sunday
Went to Church, called at Wheatleys after. Changed and rode to Cirencester with Syd and Dennis. Quaint old fashioned town. Dennis nearly 'done' coming back. [Dennis would be about twelve or thirteen with less leg power than ourselves.]

Myrna Loy.

Regrettably, we never saw the hounds, in or out of full cry.

A picturesque view of my wartime surroundings. (Taken from Folly Lane.)

THE SCHOOL CHORAL SOCIETY.

The School Choral Society, still in full strength in spite of evacuation handicaps, performed extracts from Haydn's oratorio, " The Creation," at the end of the Spring term. This took place in Stroud Parish Church, by kind permission of Canon Steer.

The performance was an excellent one from the musical point of view, but remarkable also for the fact that it was given by boys alone. Solos were taken by Ewen (Shell), Worrall (6th) and Hughes (4c), and the difficult organ accompaniment was sustained by Lowe (6th). The S. A. T. B. Choruses were efficiently performed and the opening Recitative was an inspiration as sung by the combined Tenors and Basses.

The performance was enjoyed by a large congregation, including the whole of the School.

Excerpt from *The Bridge The Journal of Handsworth Grammar School, Midsummer Term* 1940.

18 Monday
Helped Baggy with Syd to collect money for railway tickets. Went to Church in the evening to listen to the Choral Society present Hayden's 'Creation'. Very good presentation indeed. Really worthwhile listening to a decent piece of music for a change. Said goodbye to the Wheatleys.

19 Tuesday
Helped Baggy in the garden this morning. Tied up roses and generally pottered about. Hands are a pretty sight to behold now. A mass of scratches. Am playing football on Saturday for team we started before I was evacuated. Packed in the evening. Had half an hour's extension. [Lights out half an hour later than usual]. Everyone excited.

20 Wednesday
Repulsive coming back into Brum. What a difference exists between the clean open countryside of Stroud with its frolicking lambs and shooting buds and the filth and grime of Birmingham, the squalor, the poverty, the industry, the rows upon rows of identical shapeless houses, the washing on the line, the bustle, the "sick hurry." Whew! It's nauseating. A pall of gloom like that of smoke over the city settled over our compartment as we drew nearer.

Frank G Gaydoul   21 Wye Cliff Rd Birmingham 20.
NORthern 3662
                        27th March 1940.

Dear Armstrong,

             For Your information I'm N O T

co ming back to Stroud next term but teaching

at Grove Lane.I take You know all about the

School re-opening there but not who are the masters

masters.If You want anything or want to bring or

fetch books ,You will be welcome at above address
     Best Wishes, Yours sincerely, *F.G. Gaydoul*

Postcard from F. G. Gaydoul.

*

[Recovery from this bout of nausea and semi-poetic expression was swift. Back among family and friends and neighbouring parks I was soon on the go. The three week break turned out to be a sporty one with a sports injury thrown in. Football, rowing and running, that was the stuff of holiday pleasure. That scratch football team mentioned above had prospered and become the 'Bridge F.C.' with a natty strip of white shirt and black shorts. Ad hoc 'kick abouts' took place in the parks, some Stroud hardened youngsters joining in, including Shaw and Coe. Plying the oars on local pools brought great fun and frolic. So did running practice in the company of Johnnie and his younger brother Trevor, with the school sports in mind. On the last session I badly twisted an ankle and for several days, I had to come down the stairs at home, as the diary records, 'on my bottle and glass.'

Other activities included the inspection, by Syd and myself of Handsworth Park. It seemed rather forlorn, the boathouse roof damaged by earlier snows and air raid shelters looking out of place. We also examined our school which was undergoing change including the building of walls outside some classrooms as protection against possible bomb blast. On Easter Monday, Eddie and I took a train from Perry Barr to Dudley to marvel at the modernistic zoo. We both bemoaned the lack of girl-friends. Margaret had remembered my birthday (5 April) but after a holiday in Lynmouth the family were returning to Worcester. So informed, I mooned around our old haunts recording due melancholy in the diary; 'By all appearances they have ploughed up that field where Margaret and I ... The clumsy rude boot of the farm labourer now desecrates that hallow'd and sacred spot.' To some extent, self-mockery can ease the pain of heartache.

On the day before our return to Stroud came the news that Germany had invaded Norway and Denmark. The war was growing and spreading. More and more people were exchanging civilian clothes for uniforms. My friend Evan, coming up to nineteen said he would volunteer for the RAF shortly. My private thought was that once I had finished school, I should earn a bob or two, to repay Mom and Dad before donning a uniform.]

Chapter 8
April 1940

9 Tuesday
...I don't mind going back again as long as there aren't too many kids.

10 Wednesday
Arrived back at Northfield quite safely. Daffodils out and buds shooting. Couldn't go in. Still fixing up beds and taking in bedding. Hell! There will be about forty boys here soon. Lindly gave us an essay he is going to be a little different from old Sam. Terrible in the evening. Fags everywhere. Seething, swarming mass. [Sammy Gaydoul, senior teacher of German had returned to Birmingham. Mr Lindley, a younger, stricter and better teacher took over. See also p.101]

11 Thursday
Learnt today that the sports will be held a fortnight from today. Not much time to do any serious training. Shall have Trevor to beat this year and Pigott. Whew! It's going to be a tough job. What a come down these canteen dinners are. Again their contents are questionable. Going to start training tomorrow morning. [In 1939, I had been the senior champion and John Trevor, a younger boy, had won the Intermediate Championship. There was also a Junior championship. The unappetising canteen may have been one of the three British restaurants in Stroud. These restaurants resulted from a government initiative to make sure that everyone was adequately nourished. Cheap meals could be bought at what were really modest canteens. Further comments follow.]

12 Friday
Went running up Folly Lane with Davenport and Dennis. Ran right to top of lane, through woods, fields and farmyards. Most enjoyable. Had a good wash down when I got back. Went running in the evening with Davenport over Grange Fields. I am leaving a space in future for war news of momentous note.

13 Saturday
Went up Folly Lane with Davenport and Green. We ran up and down lane to farm several times. Rotten having to go to school in afternoon.

Handsworth Grammar School,

At   Marling School,

Stroud.

22nd April, 1940.

My dear Parents,

I am sure you will be happy to know that the
School has settled down quite happily for the Summer term.
There have been many rumours as to what is to happen in the
future, both at Stroud and in Birmingham.   At the moment,
there is absolutely nothing official to my knowledge regard-
ing any change in the evacuation policy.   You may rely upon
me to let you know immediately I am so advised.

From the many letters and talks I have had
with parents I know you appreciate all the difficulties of
administration, and would not wish to add to our problems.
I ask you, therefore, not to appeal to me for any changes
during the term.   Our work will be better done and our minds
set free by knowing exactly where we stand, and re-ensuring a
stabilized position for the summer term.   Towards the end
of the term I shall be writing you again, and asking your
wishes with regard to place of education.   You will then be
quite free to choose Stroud or Birmingham.   During the term,
however, I cannot make any changes.   It may well be that
the next few weeks will solve our problems for us, but I shall
feel bound to stand by the Government policy, whatever is
decided.   I deeply appreciate all you have done in establishing
a good solid front, in accordance with the Government wishes.
The unity of the School, procured by voluntary effort, is a
matter for commendation.   It expresses the right attitude and
is an answer in a small way to a thoroughly debased enemy.

I shall be glad if you will send along tuition
and sports fees by Monday next, the 29th April, where this has
not already been done.

I should like to have seen you at the School
Athletic Sports on Thursday next, but I feel sure the boys
will enjoy the contest.

With every good wish to each one of you and
your families.

I am,

Yours sincerely,

J. J. Walton
Headmaster.

The letter my parents received at the start of the summer term, 1940.

Another batch of the 'underfed'. When all youthful groups were in motion together, 'seething, swarming mass' seemed a fair description.

Stroud, from Grange fields.

14 Sunday

Beautiful day again. Spring has certainly come at last. Went to Painswick and from Painswick to Bulls Cross, Slad, woods and Folly Lane with Syd, Merriman, Godding and Quance. A most exhilarating walk.

15 Monday

Went to the Marling Playing Fields this morning and did some training. Three fast laps. I think I shall enter for the same as last year. ¼, Mile and Long Jump. Trevor entering same three for championship. Had a bath. A real treat. First one since I have been at Northfield.

16 Tuesday

Went training again this morning. R. A. S. Rees came yesterday and he seems to have settled down quite O.K. Wish we had better meals at the canteen and at Northfield. It's proper humdrum.

17 Wednesday

Went training ... did a fast quarter and heaved my heart up. Joe the silly big lug won't give us tomorrow off in order to watch the Marling Sports. As if an afternoon would make much difference to our education.

18 Thursday

Joe gave us from the second period onwards free to watch the Marling School sports. Terrible afternoon. Dull, overcast, leaden sky and an incessant drizzle. Marling sports very poor compared with our splendid function. No music. No times given. No enthusiasm as at our sports. On the whole an exceedingly poor show. I timed their senior quarter a 67 seconds. Pretty poor.

19 Friday

Went running ... behind in writing up this diary. The atmosphere of Northfield is not at all congenial to writing one's diary. Haven't the foggiest notion as to what happened in the afternoon or in the evening.

20 Saturday

Once again went running ... in the evening fetched coke to stoke hole with Ras and Syd, then played table tennis. [A curious mix of activities but at least I was expanding my stoking abilities.]

22 Monday

Last training spin. I doubt very much whether I shall be able to beat Trevor. He is supposed to have done a quarter in under 57 secs. Some accomplishment if it's true. In any case I honestly think and believe that Trevor is a better runner than I am. Had a letter from Margaret this morning. Actually sent me a photograph at last! Not a very good one but it will do for the time being. [There was a great mass of tumbled rocks to be seen but little of Margaret].

23 Tuesday
Heats today. Long jump also. Trevor won as I expected. He did 17 ft 2" and beat me by 2". Poor jump but as good as could be expected from such a rotten jumping pit. Run up uneven and not long enough. Take off board not wide enough and invisible until you were right on top of it. [That might sound like the moan of an ungracious loser. Not so, more likely a fair appraisal given my experiences at the HGS jumping pit]. Going to be a struggle between Trevor and Pigott for championship. Pigott stands a very good chance. Should win 100 and 200 yds easily. Johnnie is his only danger.

24 Wednesday
No running but went to P.T. Pigott arrived in the evening. He is in my room. Not a bad kid. Worked in the garden in the evening and then tried to play tennis. Terrible player. Can't even hit the ball, and when I do hit it, it spins off in some eccentric flight. Still I am determined to learn in order to play Margaret some time. [It was a spat over her membership of a Handsworth tennis club that had led to our 'bust-up'. One day, I thought, I will be able to afford long white flannels, but that wasn't the only component of the emotional explosion.]

25 Thursday
Went to Batemans early this morning in order to obtain shot gun. [Schoolboy lapse or exaggeration – nothing too Freudian. The 'weapon' was a starting pistol.] Sports much better staged than the Marling. Real enthusiasm. Trevor beat me in Quarter. 57 1/5. Good time. Trevor just beat me in mile after a splendid race. Just pipped me on post after I had led all the way. Glad Trevor won championship. He has won Junior and Inter cups. Best runner in school, honestly speaking. [Pity I didn't remember the Kipling line; 'You're a better man than I am Gunga Din!']

26 Friday
Baggy and Mrs Baggy gave us a decent supper in their room. What a luxury to taste a bit of cheese again. Poor old Johnnie to have his boil lanced tomorrow morning. Hope he gets on O.K. [The 'us' probably referred to the old sweats, Syd and Alf. As to the boil, I can't remember its location.]

27 Saturday
Rotten working in school. Nearly fell asleep during History. Relieved to see that parcel containing my clean washing had arrived when I got back. Played table tennis all the evening.

28 Sunday
Went the best walk I have been for years this morning. Through woods in the mist. Delicate lacery of verdant young sprays entrancing. How vast is Nature. How grand. How petty is man, how trivial. [Discuss, a possible exam question?]

THE SCHOOL SPORTS.

Held on Thursday, April 25th, at the Marling School, before a gathering from which parents and old boys were of necessity absent, the School Sports proved a great success. The weather was very favourable, the arrangements were quite adequate, and the programme ran its course amidst great enthusiasm and with no dull moments. There were no House Championship events this year, but the three Inter Form Relay Races proved that the spirit of rivalry is as keen as ever, and we hope that these events will be included in future programmes.

As a full list of results is appended, it is unnecessary to take them in detail.

Coe must be congratulated for winning the Junior Championship.

Langford, by some very good performances, secured the Intermediate Championship.

Trevor succeeded in winning the Senior Championship, and he well deserved it!

RESULTS.

100 YARDS, under 14.—1, Coe; 2, Gibbons; 3, Jones. Time: 12 2/5 secs.

100 YARDS, Intermediate—1, Hibell; 2, Millichip; 3, Murphy. Time: 11 4/5 secs.

THE BRIDGE 13

100 YARDS, Senior—1, Pigott; 2, Tookey; 3, Archer.
    Time: 11 3/5 secs.

LONG JUMP, Junior—1, Coe; 2, Sutton and Brazil. Distance: 13ft. 1½ins.

THROWING THE JAVELIN, Intermediate—1, Whitelaw; 2, Davenport; 3, Gibbons. Distance: 109ft. 7ins.

100 YARDS HANDICAP, under 13—1, Hauser; 2, Startin; 3, Sutton (1A). Time: 13 2/5 secs.

PUTTING THE 8LB. SHOT, Senior—1, Merriman; 2, Green; 3, Ralls. Distance: 40ft. 5ins.

220 YARDS, under 14 (Junior Championship)—1, Coe; 2, Massey; 3, Gibbons. Time: 28 3/5 secs.

220 YARDS, Intermediate—1, Hibell; 2, Millichip; 3, Murphy. Time: 27 3/5 secs.

220 YARDS, Senior—1, Pigott; 2, Tookey; 3, Green. Time: 26 4/5 secs.

LONG JUMP, Senior—1, Trevor; 2, Armstrong; 3, Lewis. Distance: 17ft. 2ins.

HIGH JUMP, Junior—1, Gibbons; 2, Boyes. Height: 3ft. 8ins.

INTER FORM RELAY RACE—1, 1B; 2, 1A; 3, 1C. Time: 3 mins. 19 4/5 secs.

QUARTER MILE, Senior—1, Trevor; 2, Armstrong; 3, Dee. Time: 57 1/5 secs.

HALF MILE, Intermediate—1, Langford; 2, Davenport; 3, Worrall. Time: 2 mins. 21 secs.

THROWING THE JAVELIN, Senior—1, Tookey; 2, Ralls; 3, Merriman. Distance: 116ft. 6ins.

Above may be those magical misty woods.

View from 'Paradise' Painswick.

29 Monday
Went to Batemans to buy table tennis bats and balls. Tripe game of cricket. Pitch terrible. A real storybook village green pitch. Daisies, dandelions and sheep excretion. In the evening we moved trestles and board into a spare room to furnish means for private study for Ras, Syd and I. Much better than having to put up with terrible chatter in Dining Room. Can now devote myself to some real hard work.

30 Tuesday
Hope I can hear from home soon saying I can go home for Whitsun. [It was not an issue of permission but finance – the cost of a return ticket, coach or train]. At home I shall certainly be able to stuff myself on some real good food, which will be an extremely pleasant change. Syd, Ras and I given a scone after lights out. Boy what a treat! What a luxury.

Chapter 9

May 1940

1 Wednesday
Went to P.T. Gosh! Did Sally put us through some stiff exercises. [Sally? Yes, Sally, nickname for Mr S. R. Shepherd a young teacher who helped out with gym work. He married on 20 July at St Lawrences, Stroud.] My stomach muscles are nearly wrenched out of place. Curse! We are to be turned out of our private study room because a maid is coming to live in, because Phyllis is leaving. Oh damn! damn! damn ! [To make things clear, it was not the departure of Phyllis that annoyed me but the loss of our quiet study room.] Pumped in the evening. Tough work! [On occasion, it was necessary to replenish the water supply in this traditional way.]

2 Thursday
Carried a lot of coke from stables to stoke-hole. Nothing happened at school. Played table tennis in the evening, then Baggy stopped us for having the light on. Suspended for a week now. Had one or two games of Solo. Quite a change to have a game of cards. Mom wants me to go home Whitsun.

3 Friday
Had a game of tennis. Syd in his oil tot now he can potter about in the greenhouse. Going to get some seeds tonight. Helped 'Wesser' [Mr Western, teacher of Geography] after school with National Saving Stamps. Have joined the scheme myself. Put shilling down to start with.

4 Saturday
Beautiful day. Warm and sunny. Cool and pleasant breeze. Seemed absolute sacrilege to have to go to school. [There is a very natural antipathy towards Saturday afternoon classes.] Tennis in the evening then a ride with Syd and Pigott, had previously borrowed Choobe's bike. Went nearly to Bristol Road through Stonehouse. Very pleasant.

5 Sunday
Called at the Wheatleys. Glad to see them again. Mr W quite well, Mrs, very. Going there some time to have a real meal. Went a grand ride in the afternoon, with Syd, Ras, Pigott and Barrett. Through Cranham Woods. Delightful country and weather.

Stonehouse High Street.

Cranham Woods.

Cranham.

6 Monday
Cricket this morning. Terrible game. Seven ducks terrible. Grass too wet. Saw
Johnnie's girl properly for the first time. The lucky fellow.

7 Tuesday
Nothing happened at school. Fierce debate in House of Commons over
Government's policy, especially over our failures and gross miscarrying of our
campaign in Norway. Chamberlain getting it 'in the neck'. Hope he gets kicked
out of office. Stiff-necked humbugging old fool! Trying to win the war by means
of an umbrella instead of rifle. We want the gloves off to fight a man like Hitler.
[The Prime Minister was often shown carrying a rolled up umbrella and this had
become a symbol of appeasement.]

8 Wednesday
Played tennis with Syd ... twenty one games in a row. Beat him 14-7. Went to P.T.
and had a jolly good game of skittleball. Should be very fit as I have plenty of
strenuous exercise. Dennis bought my bus ticket this dinner-time. Half price 4/6.
Shall have to have a good shave on Friday in order to diddle the Bus Company.
Good many of the boys over sixteen going back on the bus for half-price. What a
racket. Debate finished in Commons. Vote of confidence in Government's policy
carried. 281-200 circa. A pity, I am disappointed. Still Chamberlain has been
severely shaken. [I can't remember the first time my lathered downy chin was
scraped by a razor, an important part of the transition from boy to youth.]

9 *Thursday*

No letter from Margaret yet. Wonder how many times I have written that despairing phrase. Played one or two games of lawn tennis. Shall have to buy a racquet at Whitsun, then I shan't have to keep borrowing those of other boys. Presented Phyllis with lemon-set to which most of Northfield boys had contributed. Made a little speech. Quite successful. She seemed very gratified. Pleased. Went to the Ritz afterwards, with Dennis, Barrett, Griff, Madely, Heath. Had some chips coming home. [I think, though I am not sure, that the lemon-set may have consisted of a glass jug and a number of glass tumblers and maybe a bottle of lemon squash.]

10 *Friday*

Stap me!* Momentous news this morning. Holland and Belgium have now been invaded by Nazis. Stap me! It seems that the war so long awaited will now actually break out. We are going to their aid immediately. Hooray! General roll-call. Joe didn't want us to go home. Said we could return tomorrow. Nobody will I bet. Went to the baths** afterwards with Choobe and Johnnie. Delightful. Really first class baths. Really grand riding home in a coach. Managed a half-fare O.K. Most delightful journey along leafy lanes. Grand to see Mom and Dad again. Both seem fairly well though tired. At last, the long expected thrill of tucking in to a real Good meal. Grand, luscious, succulent. Fetching Nazi planes down by dozens. [* The catch phrase, regularly uttered by Reilly Ffoull , an absolute bounder, in a humorous strip cartoon of The *Daily Mirror*. **The baths in Stratford Park, Stroud.]

*

[11 *Saturday*, 12 *Sunday*, 13 *Monday*, 14 *Tuesday*, Diary entries for this short Whitsun break were much occupied with the invasion of the Low Countries. An entry that had a direct connection with life in Stroud read; 'Went to Spaldings and bought my [tennis] racquet. A last year's model which should have been 25/- but which he let me have for 15/-. Also bought a press.' Both articles, well used but undamaged are still resting in my present home.]

*

15 *Wednesday*

Had some fun on the journey. Rained with frightful velocity as we were nearing Stroud. Syd and Rees came back yesterday in compliance with Government's wishes. Didn't have to go to school until four o'clock.

16 *Thursday*

Can't play tennis because the court is unfit for hard wear. Wants a jolly good rest. Brown parched earth at either end of court.

THE KEENEST BLADE IS CHADE
3 HOLE & SLOTTED £.2.3
OBTAINABLE EVERYWHERE

Evening Standard

Amusements 10
Radio 10

BLACK-OUT 9.5 pm, 4.47 am.
MOON Rose 7.37 am; Sets 11.24 pm.

No. 36,093   LONDON, FRIDAY, MAY 10, 1940   ONE PENNY

NAZIS INVADE HOLLAND, BELGIUM, LUXEMBURG: MANY AIRPORTS BOMBED

Allies Answer Call for Aid: R.A.F. Planes are in Action

HITLER HAS INVADED HOLLAND, BELGIUM AND LUXEMBURG. HIS PARACHUTE TROOPS ARE LANDING AT SCORES OF POINTS AND MANY AIRPORTS ARE BEING BOMBED.

THE DUTCH HAVE OPENED THEIR FLOODGATES AND CLAIM TO HAVE BROUGHT DOWN A DOZEN BOMBERS.

It was confirmed in official quarters in London shortly after 8a.m. to-day that appeals for assistance have been received from both the Belgian and Dutch Governments, and that these Governments have been told that H.M. Government will, of course, render all the help they can.

Every airport in Belgium has been attacked by Nazi airplanes, it is announced in Brussels.

BRUSSELS IS BEING "BOMBARDED TERRIFICALLY," SAYS A NEW YORK MESSAGE.

A Zurich report states that casualties in the first raid over Brussels amounted to 400 dead and wounded.

Lyons Airport Bombed

Other reports say that Antwerp and the airport at Lyons (France) have been bombed.

THE BELGIAN ARMY IS RESISTING THE GERMAN INVASION, IT IS OFFICIALLY ANNOUNCED IN PARIS. GENERAL MOBILISATION HAS BEEN PROCLAIMED.

BRUSSELS RADIO ANNOUNCE THAT ALLIED TROOPS ARE ON THE WAY TO BELGIUM'S AID.

French, Belgian and British airplanes have been sighted over Holland, states an official Dutch announcement.

"These airplanes," it was added, "belong to our Allies and they are enthusiastically greeted as a sign of friendship."

Military Airfields +
Civil +
Seaplane Bases ▲
0   30 MILES

NORTH SEA

Texel
De Mok
De Kooy
Schellingwoude
Amsterdam
The Hague
Schiphol
Ypenburg
Rotterdam
Waalhaven
Haamstede
Veere
Gilze Rijen
Flushing

Leeuwarden
Eelde

ZUIDER ZEE

Bussum
Oldebroek
Twente
Teuge
Milligen
Soesterberg
Arnhem
Vucht
Eindhoven
Venlo

G E R M A N Y

B E L G I U M
Brussels
Aachen

34

The Dutch Legation in London announce:
"Our appeal for aid sent to the Allied Governments has been answered. Britain and France are going to our assistance immediately."

Belgium, too, appealed for help. The Luxemburg Government have fled.

(Continued on PAGE TWO)

HITLER IS FOLLOWING THE SCHLIEFFEN PLAN—SPECIAL ARTICLE AND MAP, PAGE SEVEN.

You Must Carry Your Gas Mask

A.R.P. Should Be On Alert

—Says Ministry

The Minister of Home Security states that in the light of to-day's events in Holland and Belgium, it is very necessary that all civil defence and A.R.P. services should be on the alert.

The carrying of gas masks by the public is once more necessary. They should acquaint themselves with the position of shelters and first aid post in their neighbourhoods.

Householders are recommended to overhaul their domestic preparations against air attack.

Anti-aircraft guns over a wide area around the mouth of the Thames were in action at dawn to-day when five German airplanes, believed to be Heinkel bombers, flew over the coast and passed over several towns.

The sound of heavy firing awakened thousands of people, who hurriedly dressed and went into the streets to catch a glimpse of the raiders.

No air raid warning was sounded, but wardens were on duty and shepherded everyone indoors.

Five airplanes, flying in an arrowhead formation, were seen. They were flying at about 10,000 feet. Their course was clearly marked by the puffs and flashes of the bursting shells from the anti-aircraft batteries.

They were flying due east. A few

(Continued on Back Page, Col. Three)

The German advance continues.

Just Jake, A popular *Daily Mirror* cartoon strip.

The swimming pool at Stratford Park.

17 Friday

Went to the baths at nine o'clock. Most enjoyable. Water rather cold but that did little to minimise the pleasures to be derived from swimming. We intend some morning to play tennis after coming out of the baths. Nothing happened at school. Germans advancing all the while. Went to the Ritz in the evening with Syd and Rees. Spent 1/8. Stap me!

18 Saturday

For the very first time I broke my Saturday night ruling, and did some homework. Helped along with the rest of the boys on our table, some chappie to carry chairs from Uplands Institute to the Church. Quite diverting. Greatly surprised at the size and beauty of church, which from distant external appearances I had judged to be

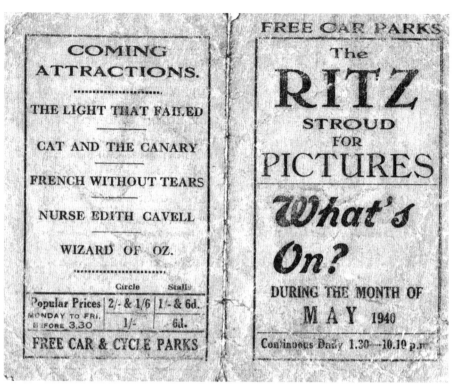

Above and below: The modern, rather swish Ritz cinema had opened in 1939.

Painswick church.

rather freakish.

19 Sunday

Really marvellous Summer day. Pergot*, Syd , Ras and I shot out of Stroud on bikes in the afternoon through Painswick. Sat by the wayside and played cards. Fun! Really delightful to feel warm sun on one's face after months of chilly depressing weather. [Just a touch of schoolboy hyperbole in the last remark. *Pigott]

20 Monday

Dried up with Syd and 'Bert' Madely this morning. Great fun pulling old Madely's leg. Terrible slacker. Made a dive for all the knives, forks, spoons, eggcups etc and then spent too long on them. [A shrewd fellow, Bert, bagging all the smaller items and playing for time.] Went to cricket afterwards. Made a magnificent 11. Nothing happened at school. Ras going to London to sit for Wakefield Scholarship. Been pulling his leg about Delia Daroux the person where he is staying.

21 Tuesday

Met Johnnie and went with Ras and Syd to Stratford Park. Excellent hard courts. Well worth ninepence to enjoy an hours refreshing and invigorating game. Nothing happened at school. Stopped in all evening and worked solidly at German and French proses.

22 Wednesday

Almost late again this morning for P.T. We have again that fat – for master. [The name is under wraps out of a sense of fair play]. Gosh does he look ghastly in a gym rigout. Great rolls of bulging fat resting everwhere. Ticked us off, or rather the hint that there would be trouble if we were not more punctual. Nothing happened at school. [That was a regular refrain]. Ras has departed for London now. I wonder how he will get on with Delia. [Girls with exotic names were beyond, well beyond, my experience. Delia may have been plump, plain and elderly, but it's great to fantasise, just occasionally.]

23 Thursday

Mowed old Syd down 6-0 6-2. That larn't him. Baggy going ahead to make us fluent & conversant in French. Great fun to listen to Syd's and Johnnie's hesitations and falterings but not half so funny when it is my turn. Heard from Mom this morning. At last I have some money. Have been on the rocks for the past few days but I have some money owing to me. [Pity I can't remember who from.]

24 Friday

Went to the Baths this morning and had quite a good swim. Went home and then had another bath, should be clean as clean can be by now. Serious news. Learnt in school that Boulogne has fallen. Stap me! We certainly seem to have our backs against the wall. I hope I can see Margaret on Sunday. Dennis says they might possibly come down if they can obtain the petrol. [Petrol rationing had been in operation for several months.]

Serious students alfresco.

The Gables, Painswick.

The stocks in Painswick.

The Golden Heart, Painswick.

Rowers on the Avon at Tewkesbury.

25 *Saturday*
Rotten working at school as usual on a Saturday afternoon. Can't remember what happened in the evening.

26 *Sunday*
Went a walk with Merrimans [twins] after Church. Dennis' folk didn't come in the afternoon.

27 *Monday*
Felt extremely annoyed this morning. Court is absent so Baggy asked me to take his form. Had to look after 4B. Quite alright but made me miss part of my game of cricket. At school in the afternoon. Joe as boring as usual. How his periods give me the willies. Writing down your thoughts. Just sheer damn hypocrisy. We only write down what we should think if we were moved by the Spirit in so short a space of time. [Rather convoluted, but I think it means that we fudged this 'spiritual' task.]

28 *Tuesday*
There is a great deal of revision to be done. One most important thing that I forgot to put down in my diary last Friday, and which I must note here is the fact that I received a letter, or rather two in one envelope from Margaret. Very pleasant letters. Can see her this Sunday at Tewkesbury. Have replied saying that I can & will. Gosh how I hope that the weather will be a little better than it is today.

Super Creamy Super Cleansing
CREMEX SHAMPOO

BLACK-OUT
ZERO
HOUR
TO-NIGHT
UNTIL 4.21 A.M.
MOON MOON
RISES SETS

Daily Express

No. 12,487   Friday, May 31, 1940   One Pe

Through an inferno of bombs and shells the B.E.F. is crossi the Channel from Dunkirk—in history's strangest armada

TENS OF THOUSANDS
SAFELY HOME ALREAD

Many more coming by day and night

SHIPS OF ALL SIZES DARE THE GERMAN GUNS

UNDER THE GUNS OF THE BRITISH FLEET, UNDER THE WINGS OF THE ROYAL AIR FORCE, A LARGE PROPORTION OF THE B.E.F. WHO FOR THREE DAYS HAD BEEN FIGHTING THEIR WAY BACK TO THE FLANDERS COAST, HAVE NOW BEEN BROUGHT SAFELY TO ENGLAND FROM DUNKIRK.

First to return were the wounded. An armada of ships—all sizes, all shapes—were used for crossing the Channel. The weather which helped Hitler's tanks to advance has since helped the British evacuation.

Cost to the Navy of carrying out, in an inferno of bombs and shells, one of the most magnificent operations in history has been three destroyers, some auxiliary craft, and a small steamer.

Cost to the enemy of the Fleet's intervention outside Dunkirk can be counted in the shattering of

How the Allies fought back to Dunkirk, aided by warships and planes. British troops held the left flank, French troops the right flank. Last rear- | guard action (see inset) fought by Fre General Prioux on the hills between O Ypres

Tired, dirty, hungry they came back —unbeatable

—THREE—
DESTROYERS
LOST

As Navy helps B.E.F.

Signpo to be remov

SIR JOHN REITH Transport

The 'Dunkirk spirit' shines through in this article.

29 Wednesday
Early for P. T. Had a good game of skittleball. Innes [teacher] certainly put us thro' the exercises. It seems that our B.E.F. is cut off in Belgium. Stap me! [B.E.F. was the British Expeditionary Force.]

30 Thursday
Feel rather stiff this morning after all those fearful exercises of yesterday. (*Weedon brought the news that the Belgian army has capitulated under orders from King Leopold. The hound. Ought to be shot for such an act. Government say they will carry on despite the action of the King. All these noble utterances of fighting shoulder to shoulder to the last man and then he goes and commits an action unparalleled in history. * This happened on Tuesday.) Broke Ras' bed in the evening. Most funny episode though it will cost us 3/- and had a practice air raid warning. 1.30 am. Pretty good.

31 Friday
Felt rather under the weather this morning. Pains in my neck. Baggy and Mrs B half afraid that I have got the mumps, but I am positive that this is not the case. Had a postcard from Margaret saying that she can see me on Sunday 11-15 at Tewkesbury. Am determined at all costs to be there. Am not going to have one day so eagerly looked forward to, spoiled by the fussiness of Mr & Mrs B. Felt much better in the evening. [Clearly, I could be a headstrong blighter and harsh in my judgements. I plead youth and ignorance in mitigation. I was also becoming slipshod in my diary keeping as some of the entries show. For this slackness, I can think of many possible reasons but all I will offer now is a saying of the Tommies of the First World War – 'San Fairy Ann' a good natured attempt at 'ca ne faire rien' – it doesn't matter.]

Chapter 10

June 1940

1 Saturday

Worked in the morning ... afternoon ... evening for a little while. Ras and myself drew up scheme for Table Tennis Tournament for the whole of Northfield. Under 14 and over 14. Two prizes for each class. Syd and Pergot went down town to purchase provisions for tomorrows ride. They are going with Ras & Archer to Bourton on Water.

2 Sunday

A grand day. Put on cycling jacket and set off at 9. Met Margaret at 11-10 only had to wait 5 mins. Rode to Twyning, sat in a field for hours ate our dinner and lay and dreamed. Then rode to Tewkesbury and rowed on the Severn for an hour. Moored under the willows and had tea. Set back at 6. Most enjoyable day. One of the best ever. As she grows older Margaret improves which is saying a lot. Charming girl. See her again after exams in about six or seven weeks time. These meetings after long periods of separation seem sweeter. A really magnificent day. Pleasant companion ship, delightful company. [Away from this idyllic setting and mood, beyond our imagination and way beyond our comprehension, British and Allied troops were still being evacuated from the beaches of Dunkirk, some 26,000 on this particular day.]

3 Monday

Cricket this morning. It really is flaming June. Nothing happened at school except that we were bored to tears again by Joe. Played my game against Davenport in the evening and beat him 21-15 (rec 5) and passed into the second round. Joe told us that Oral French would be held on 24 June, Edmund St Brum. Given us a weekend off Yippee!

4 Tuesday

Must get down to serious revision now. Glad that we cannot play tennis due to the worn condition of the court. Our principle distraction has been painlessly removed. Baggy put us through some gruelling and annoying oral practice. Dicky Rees went to London again today for an interview but came back the same evening.

5 Wednesday

P.T. this morning then went out into the open field and played Rugby Touch. Much better than playing skittleball in the dull, dim gym. Beautiful hot day again. Cloudless pastel blue sky.

A relaxing afternoon on the Avon.

Although the Dunkirk evacuation constituted a triumph of a life rescuing kind, great masses of arms and equipment had to be left behind. Such losses had to be made good by the heroic efforts of British factory workers, men and women, and American help.

'There's nothing like a cuppa cha!' Soldiers returning from Dunkirk.

6 Thursday

Life seems to be all work now. Hitler has launched a great new offensive in the West. Certainly had us beaten in Holland & Belgium. Witness our forced and valiant evacuation of troops. Why must we be always at least six moves behind? It certainly seems as though we have at last entered into a life and death struggle. Praise God we come through it victorious.

7 Friday

Went to the Baths this morning. Another glorious day with the sun scorching down. Lovely in the water and equally pleasant sunbathing. Had an extremely pleasant surprise when I arrived back. Found beside a letter and Birmingham Mail from Mother which is always welcome, a letter from Margaret. So soon, and without my having written to her. Intended writing today. Very nice letter. She suffered unfortunate mishaps on the way back in form of a puncture. There was an X on back of envelope. H'm I wonder! Feel very bucked. Wrote to her in the evening and had a feed of radishes and bread & butter.

8 Saturday

Letter from home with remittance. Gone up to 3/- now. Heard welcome news that Dad has at last obtained a settled job. At a munitions factory, interrogating people as they enter the gates. Suit him down to the ground. Awful at school this afternoon doing a History Test while Marling School were playing cricket just outside in the glorious sunshine.

9 Sunday

No church this morning for a pleasant change. Wrote English essay and then larked about. Gymnastics and fights galore. Heard from Dennis that Margaret might come down and stay at Bear Inn for few days with her Mom and Dad. [No ecstatic reaction recorded in diary – I did retain a sceptical streak.]

10 Monday

Dull dark overcast, mist all over the hills. Presage of thunder and rain but none came. Played cricket despite the wet conditions. We were spared the delightful pleasure of Joe for Divinity this afternoon. Chap in the neighbouring gardens told us some astounding news. Italy has declared war on the Allies. Confirmed on nine o'clock news. Stirring speech by Duff-Cooper full of optimism for the future. Spoke a great deal of forceful home truths about Italy. Famous for its ruins! Will be more so in future. He really larn'd 'em and I hope we take initiative. [Duff-Cooper had been appointed by Winston Churchill to be Minister of Information. Many people still remembered the Italians' use of mustard gas during Mussolini's war against Abyssinia (Ethiopia) 1935-6.]

11 Tuesday

Well today war with Italy starts. Wonder what will happen. Beautiful weather continuing but I fervidly hope that it does not continue like this through the course of exams. Robs one's ability for power of thinking. Thoughts become confused and muddled. Germans creeping nearer Paris. Stap me! Nothing we do seems to be able to stop them.

The Bear Hotel, Stroud.

On 10 May 1940 Winston Churchill became the prime minister, heading a coalition government. He was to make many stirring speeches.

Ronald Colman.

12 *Wednesday*
Germans still creeping towards Paris. 16 miles away. Mom has written to Joe asking him if I can go home on the bus as it is cheaper. As he did not send for me in the course of the afternoon went to see him at break. Gave me and John & Syd extra half-day off with pleasure. In a most affable mood. Must have enjoyed his stay in Brum. [Savouring creature comforts?] Well tomorrow I'll be at home again. Yippee! A long rest and some decent meals, and above all the welcome sight of Mom and Dad again. Wonder how Dad likes his new job. Was overjoyed when I heard the news.

13 *Thursday*
Germans still nearer to Paris. Attempting and succeeding again with outflanking movements. Learned that bus was not til 3-30 so went to the Ritz with Syd for a couple of hours to see *The Light that Failed*. For sheer acting one of best pictures I have yet seen. Ronald Colman excellent. Bus behind us broke down. Had to

transfer passengers to ours. Necessitated my sitting on Johnnie's and Syd's knees [I was a notably a bit shorter than my pals] and standing up. [Not on their knees.] Barricades all along roads. Stopped several times for Identity Cards. Good to see Mom and Dad again, though Dad tired out by his job. Too much standing, coupled with heat and gammy leg. Curse this War!

14 Friday

Stap me. Paris has fallen. Hope to God French don't give up fighting. Grand to stop in bed till nine o'clock, and have a real breakfast of bacon & egg, and real marmalade. Magnificent. Went up to University, Edmund Street, for Oral Examination in French. Worked on *La France et les Français* in the evening. Seems a little ironic.

15 Saturday

Germans driving deeper & deeper into French territory. Cutting off Maginot Line. Reynaud appealed to Roosevelt. Sending us all possible material aid short of an expeditionary force. We have had successes in Libya. Captured two forts. In desperation we have bombed Essen & German industrial towns. No more than we should have done in beginning of war. [The Maginot Line consisted of a long stretch of massive concrete fortification on the eastern frontier of France. Its purpose was to deter a German invasion. But as the Belgians would not allow the wall to be continued along their frontier with Germany, the Germans invaded the Low Countries, so rendering the vaunted Maginot Line useless. Paul Reynaud was the Prime Minister of France.]

16 Sunday

Worked on *La France et les Français*. Finished it. A most studious weekend.

17 Monday

Set back for Stroud with John and Syd at eleven o'clock. Had some fun with a funny old spinster on the bus. One continual plaintive moan all the way down. Not enough air, too many stops etc. Got out at Painswick minus her ear trumpet. A

Paris falls to the 'Nazi jackboot'!

National identity card, every person was required to carry one.

most valuable instrument, worth at least twenty pounds. Fished under the seat and dragged out a huge block used for stopping bus on hills. Such fun. Terrible news. France has asked for an armistice. Stap me!

18 Tuesday

Fighting still going on in France. Germans advancing rapidly. Hitler to meet Mussolini. Back to the old grind again in the afternoon. Stap me! What a come down from working at home. Still it is good to see the faces of the fellow inhabitants of Northfield again. Listened to complaints lodged by smaller fry of my bedroom against the ruthless discipline of Pergot. Hope he larnt 'em. I know what they are.[Pergot had military experience – see below.]

19 Wednesday

P.T. in the morning and rugby touch. Letter from Margaret. Again agreeably surprised in her writing so soon. Curse – she may have to be moved to Coalville, a dirty mining hole not far from Ashby de la Zouch. Shall have to see her before she does move. Planned evacuation of children 6-16 to Dominions.

20 Thursday

One thing I have forgotten to inscribe in Monday's page is the fact that Glyn Davies late of 5C has come down to join us. We were 4 now we are 5. More raids on British coast. French still fighting. Germans occupied Lyons. S. Wales bombed.

21 Friday

Went to the Baths this morning. Had a little tiff with Baggy before I went. He wanted me to take a form again while he went to hospital. I refused as I had already done it twice. Syd Sharpley has not done it once yet. Baths very cold. Biting wind. No one stopped in more than half an hour. Went down the chute for the first time. Quite good. Magnificent sensation. Wrote a letter to Margaret. Germany handed over armistice terms to France. Not yet published. [Because I wish not to be judged too harshly on limited evidence, Mr Lindon's hospital visit was probably concerned with his being escort to a young schoolboy needing medical attention.]

22 Saturday

Worked in the afternoon but became a little fed up so went with Syd Sharpley up to the woods and had some fun with Scat Saunders' gun. Horrible piece of mechanism. Sights out of true. Fired about one shot in every three, but managed to pick petals off daisies (at about 10 yds). Armistice signed. Terms being considered. Troops still fighting. [The gun was an air rifle.]

23 Sunday

No Church this morning. Went up the lane and played rounders with Nery, Dick, Syd and Gus Brakewell. Worked in aft. Went a little walk with Syd and Dennis. In evening met latter's parents with Margaret. Spent a most enjoyable evening with her. Magnificent. Her parents very nice. Den being evacuated to Canada. Her parents

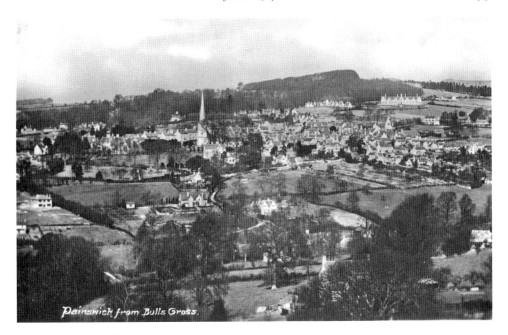

Painswick from Bulls cross.

Yet another bunch of young 'desperadoes'. The injury to the arm was probably occasioned by over exuberant larking about.

want Margaret to go. She is firmly resolved that she doesn't want to go. Don't know what to think. [The evacuation of children to overseas locations, principally Australia, Canada and the USA is a separate piece of history in its own right.]

24 Monday

Missed washing up (or rather wiping) this morning as we had an exam. English Scholarship. I thought it was quite alright. It must have been the inspiration I derived from last night's meeting. Went to the Park in the afternoon and played tennis with Syd. Had a sixpenny iced drink after. (Had 1/6 dinner too at Canteen) because we were late, sat watching the bowls players. Most peaceful, typical English summer afternoon. Did some French swotting in the evening. German terms published, French to give up army, navy & airforce to Germany & Italy. Stap me!

25 Tuesday

At five minutes to one this morning air raid warnings sounded in Stroud. Everyone bundled down to the garage & and sat dithering in pyjamas on the cold floor.

Britain now truly stands alone.

Most annoying. Lasted for nearly 2 hrs. Stiff, cold and weary we crawled back to bed again, cursing profanely at the dastardly activities of Nazi aeroplanes. My rosy illusions of yesterday afternoon completely shattered. AA [Ack- Ack] defences in action over Bristol. Planes passed over Stroud at half past 12. French Scholarship late in the morning. Pretty foul. Went to sleep on beds in afternoon. Free until next Tuesday. French ceased fighting.

26 Wednesday
Had a false air raid alarm again at five to one this morning. Went to bed about a quarter of an hr later. Been in bed about 15 mins when alarm went again. Cursing profoundly dashed downstairs and sat for another hr & ½ in garage. What a life. Not so bad tonight. Heard German planes go over. One circled over Stroud for about 10 mins before he finally pithered off. Didn't go to P.T. this morning. Felt much to tired. Terrible drag having to get up at seven. Feel like a wet rag. No panic however and everyone looks on the raids as a matter of course now. Attacked Swindon.

27 Thursday
As I thought. Stap me! Had another air raid warning this morning. Only lasted twenty minutes however. Our new shelter in passage-way. Much more cheerful. Light and able to play cards. Learned later that it was only a false alarm. With the waning of the moon doubt if any more raids will take place for some time as German bombers are afraid to attack in open daylight. Russia up to her tricks again. Ultimatum to Rumania demanding concession of Bessarabia. Seems as

The bowls green at Stratford Park.

Above , below and right: This cinema was opened in 1931 by the greatly popular British film and stage actress, singer and dancer, Jessie Matthews. But probably not in this guise.

GAUMONT PALACE, STROUD - INFORMATION AT A GLANCE

JULY ATTRACTIONS

Date	Features	Stars
MONDAY JULY 1st For 3 Days	THEY CAME BY NIGHT	Will Fyffe
	CHARLIE CHAN IN CITY IN DARKNESS	Sidney Toler
THURSDAY JULY 4th For 3 Days	THE OLD MAID	Belle Davis
	Inquest	Elizabeth Allen
MONDAY JULY 8th For 3 Days	A WINDOW IN LONDON	Michael Redgrave
	Mutiny in the Big House	Charles Bickford
THURSDAY JULY 11th For 3 Days	THE HOUSEKEEPER'S DAUGHTER	Joan Bennet
	The Forgotten Women	Sigrid Gurie
MONDAY JULY 15th For 3 Days	THE CHINESE BUNGALOW	Paul Lukas
	' SONS OF THE SEA	Leslie Banks
THURSDAY JULY 18th For 3 Days	SWISS FAMILY ROBINSON	Thomas Mitchell
	KID NIGHTINGALE	John Payne
MONDAY JULY 22nd For 3 Days	DUST BE MY DESTINY	John Garfield
	WE'RE IN THE ARMY NOW	Ritz Brothers
THURSDAY JULY 25th For 3 Days	BARRICADE	Alice Faye
	That's Right You're Wrong	Adolphe Menjou
MONDAY JULY 29th	Vigil IN THE NIGHT	Carole Lombard
	Married and in Love	Alan Marshall
THURSDAY AUG. 1st For 3 Days	LAW AND DISORDER	Leslie Banks
	Mr. Wong at Headquarters	Boris Karloff
	March of Time—No. 2	

CHILDREN'S MATINEE EVERY SATURDAY MORNING. Doors open 10.0 a.m.   SPECIAL PROGRAMME.   PRICES : 3d. and 6d.

TIMES OF PERFORMANCES — CONTINUOUS from 1.30 to 10 p.m. Doors 1.15 p.m.

PRICES OF ADMISSION (including Tax):
CHEAP MATINEE PRICES 1.30 p.m. to 3.30 p.m.

Ground Floor	...	9d.	Child	...	4d. }	Saturdays and Bank
Circle	...	1/-	Child	...	6d. }	Holidays excepted.

USUAL PRICES

Front Circle	...	2/-	Child	...	...	1/-
Back Circle and Back Stalls	...	1/	Child	...	...	9d.
Centre Stalls	...	1/-	Child	...	...	6d.
Front Stalls	...	6d.	Child	...	...	4d.

NO CHILDREN'S PRICES SATURDAY EVENINGS AND BANK HOLIDAYS.

JESSIE MATTHEWS

Park Gardens, Stroud.

Folly Lane runs at the back of the shelter on the right.

though she wants to prevent Germany from extending her influence to the Black Sea. Be a real world war soon. [The last prediction was not too far out!]

28 Friday

No air raid this morning, although I woke up at the usual time. Joyful change to be able to stop in one's bed all the allotted period. Worked hard in the morning. Mucked about in the afternoon. Went to the Gaumont in the evening. Most pleasant time had by all. Syd, Dick, Perg, Barret (Bert) and myself. Had some fun coming back. Singing, trucking about the streets. Having a runt or bolsch or donnock. 94. Rumania ceded Bessarabia. Russian troops nearly on Danube. [What I take to be curious schoolboy neologisms here. Fortunately, they did not take root. For some long forgotten reason 94 had assumed special and hilarious properties in our schoolboy lore as it operated at Northfield.]

29 Saturday

Yesterday afternoon received a letter from Mrs Wheatley telling us the sad news that Mr Wheatley passed away Wednesday evening. Best thing really as he had been bad since Christmas. Went to his funeral in the morning. Feel sorry for Mrs Wheatley. Still lives at School House. [The candour of youth can sound a little callous but that is not the intention. Limited emotional experience plays a large part in what is said or not said, done or not done.] Had terrific fights all aft. On the lawn. Filled the diary up in the evening. Poor Mrs Wheatley.

30 Sunday

This morning, this afternoon, and evening I worked. Learned quite a lot of English quotations. Most unfortunately Margaret did not come this Sunday. [The work, of course, consisted of reading, memorising and revising.]

Chapter 11

July 1940

1 Monday
Sat with Dicky Rees on the front lawn all morning and worked. Only one without an exam in the afternoon. Did a fair amount of work. Went to sleep under the warm drugging effect of the sun and the balmy air. French tomorrow all day. At five to twelve, air raid sirens blew. Lasted an hour. Just our luck. No air raids for a week then when I start [exams] they start.

2 Tuesday
Principal French this morning. Not too bad. French to English in the bag. French II in the afternoon. Shared out cake in the evening and generally messed about. Russian occupation of Bessarabia completed.

3 Wednesday
Worked all day today preparing for English Principal. Sat or rather lay on beds all afternoon. Went to sleep in the most easy fashion. Had to be wakened in order to make my doddery way to the dining room. Obtained further inspiration this evening. Sitting on the front lawn swotting when the Ds arrived in full force, bringing Dennis back from medical exam for candidates for Canada. Saw Margaret for about three minutes. Sufficient to bear me thro' the trials and tribulation of tomorrow. Magnificent. Six German planes brought down off coast.

4 Thursday
English Principal I. Not bad at all. Fear I have mis-read paper and done a question I should not have done. English II not so hot. Required too much thought, but think I have done quite well in it. News of steps being taken by the British government to prevent French fleet from falling into enemy hands. Many French warships in British hands. Dunkerque and others resisted, the hounds. Shows many influential Frenchmen have Nazi sympathies. We have sunk or damaged severely many French destroyers which put up a resistance. Went to see Wizard of Oz. Most enjoyable. [Much of the tragic naval action took place at Oran, in Libya.]

5 Friday
Swotted German all day. World wide satisfaction at Britain's action against French fleet. That'll larn those Nazis. [Most of us, certainly as schoolboys, were susceptible to our own propaganda.]

4 THE BRIDGE

IN MEMORIAM.

EDWARD JOHN BOYES, Age 12 Years.

The School was shocked and grieved to learn of the death of E. J. Boyes on the evening of 3rd July, at the Stratford Park Swimming Pool, Stroud. He entered Handsworth Grammar School in September, 1939, and became Form Captain of Ic. He was very popular with his fellows, and had shown great keenness in work and sport. Much sympathy will be felt for his parents in their irreparable loss. The School was represented at the funeral in Birmingham, and wreaths were sent from the Head Master, Staff and School, and from his Form.

E. J. Boyes memorial, featured in *The Bridge*, 1940.

Judy Garland as Dorothy, young heroine of the film.

6 Saturday
Lively discussion between Baggy and George Peck as to where the exam was to be held and Baggy's comments on George's muddling were particularly scathing. Such fun. Need not have feared German exam extremely easy, hardly a word that I did not know. Finished comfortably in two hours. Only one more exam now and that should be easy. History. Played footer in afternoon.

7 Sunday
Went a super walk after church. Round Rodborough. Called in Golden Cross, cider. Italian fleet bombed by R.A.F. Marvellous views this morning. Most enjoyable.

8 Monday
Swotted on the tennis court for the most part of the morning. History not so easy as we expected, curse it, but think I have done quite O.K. To celebrate [end of exams] Syd and I together with Hawkes buzzed off to the Gaumont. Had a special late pass. Came back and feasted upon bread, cheese and onions. Shot between the sheets at quarter to eleven after an extremely enjoyable evening.

9 Tuesday
Syd pottered off to garden frames this morning. Went to school in the afternoon where we spent a most boring time passed in the usual after examination time

Arguably the cream of the Northfield evacuees – Pigott, Rees, Sharpley and Armstrong, who had nicked his chin that morning shaving.

HGS sixth formers in a Marling School classroom – Mick Fellows, Johnnie Archer, Syd Sharpley, Alf Armstrong and young Guise, son of senior English master.

manner, reading, messing about and yawning. Walked up Selsley with Dick, Syd and Davies in the evening. Poured with rain. Huddled on the top of the hill admiring the view. Mist, distant hills, shafts of golden sunlight shooting down upon the ribbon of the Severn. The incessant silver arrows of rain. Absolutely soaked when we got back. Had a meat pie. German planes over Stroud. Bombs dropped at Hardwicke.

10 *Wednesday*
Hope I hear from Margaret soon as in two weeks time I shall be an old boy. Stap me! Rained in torrents incessantly all the afternoon. Stopped in and re-started my sketch of Bebe Daniels. Report of naval engagement with Italian fleet. Italian ships retire behind smoke screen laid by Italian destroyers. Poor lot of fighters.

11 *Thursday*
Went a walk up Rodborough this morning in order that Syd could take some infra-red photos of surrounding countryside. Syd accosted by a drayman and submitted to a scanty cross examination. Had to turn back early because of the rain. Fierce aerial battle over the Channel. Twenty-two planes brought down on our coast in one day. Hitler's Luftwaffe is finding Britain a hard nut to crack.

Rodborough Fort.

12 *Friday*

Seems to have done nothing else but rain all the week. Glad I did not write to Margaret yesterday as I received a letter from her this morning. Can see me next weekend at Tewkesbury. Yippee! Hooray. How I hope the weather clears up. Miserable morning but went to the baths with Dick & Perg. Only three there. Quite warm in the water but awful when we came out. Planning a ride to Tewkesbury on Sunday. Seven of us going. The gang of four. Bert Barret, Toob and G. Davies. [Toob is an alternative spelling of Choobe.]

13 *Saturday*

Messed about all morning. No I didn't. I wrote a letter to Margaret. Messed about at school. Joe came and told us we could have afternoon off. Wonders will never cease. Went back to Northfield where we were nabbed by Baggy and made to mark papers. Curse, curse, curse. [Our French must have been reasonable.]

14 *Sunday*

At last a beautiful day. The Gods were kind to us. Set off at 10 to 10. Rode at good speed to Tewkesbury. Had dinner in field. Went on river for an hour. Rode into Cheltenham and then up to Cranham. Marvellous views. Tried happy cider, cider.

15 *Monday*

Volunteered to take Burnell to hospital again, instead of going to cricket. Dull unsettled St Swithins. Merriman played the piano at the canteen. Table tennis

Cranham.

tournament finals in the evening. Walters beat Dennis and Dickie beat Dan both results as expected.

16 *Tuesday*

Went down to town this morning, shopping. Read *Millennium** at school in the afternoon. Baggy took Syd and I home in his car at half past four. Lucky for we escaped the rain. Parcel of food from Mom awaiting me when we reached Northfield. Cake, jelly, ** carrots etc. Bless her. What a mother. Syd, Dick, Perg, Lou and I went a good long tramp in the evening. Walked as far as Haresfield Beacon. Lovely views. Mist, hills, the Severn. Nature and the rain. I shall remember these tramps in years to come. Had some fun coming back. (She*** was poor but she was honest & etc.)

   [* At the end of the diary where I have recorded 'Books Read and Films Seen' I have written; 'Millennium, Upton Sinclair – Interesting surmise of life in 2000 depicting man's evolution through slavery, feudalism, capitalism, all ending happily in co-operative socialism.' Upton Sinclair was a prolific American author and staunch socialist. ** in cube form.*** For its day, slightly risqué, a song featuring a fair maiden, rent arrears and a dastardly squire.]

17 *Wednesday*

Wrote a letter home acknowledging the parcel and stressing the dire need for more money. Had an interview with a lady from Junevile Labour Employment Bureau. Very helpful and encouraging. Went a delightful walk in the evening with Dick, Syd, Bart B, Merriman and Johnnie. Along London Road, up over a hill onto common

Eric's 'dormitory' minus one fag smoking absentee in the shrubbery, plus adopted pal from single room, Dickie Rees. So – Madeley and Heath, Rees (who always seems to be searching out a hollow tooth?) Armstrong, Pigott and nippers Deeley and Hayward.

by Bear Inn, then through King's Court to Golden Cross, where we refuelled on cider, back along Bath Road home. Wish Jupiter Pluvius would lift his dark, heavy, sullen grey mantle from off the world.

18 Thursday

Went to the baths ... dull and miserable but quite enjoyable on the whole. Fortunate again, went home early in Baggy's car. Tidied up the tennis court. Snipping weeds mending the wire fences and etc. Should be able to play on the court tomorrow. Quite respectable, as good as new.

19 Friday

No letter from Margaret as yet. Stap me! Must be something wrong. Most probably unable to come curse it. Staff Match in the afternoon. Quite a good game. For once in many years the School won. Worrall knocked 20 N.O. and that young kid Turner played a jolly good game. Many amusing incidents while the Staff were playing. Apple's sliding tackles and sprints after the ball. Looneybin's dashes between the wickets, Westerns stance, swipe and dismissal. & etc. & etc.

20 Saturday

Letter from Margaret. As I thought waiting to see whether she could come or not. Unfortunately she cannot as friends are coming from Birmingham. Added a brief after note stating or rather inviting me to go to T, Northwick Close etc on Friday if I possibly could. Will do so most certainly if I am able. Commenced work on the *Northfield Nark*. An amusing journal* about and of interest to Northfieldites. [* While replete with schoolboy facetiousness, genuine grievances of poor quality and inadequate food are 'subtly' conveyed.]

21 Sunday
Daylight raid this morning. Only twenty minutes however. Went to Mrs Wheatleys. Seems to have recovered well. Invited to tea on Wednesday. Went with Perg & Syd to Haresfield Beacon in the afternoon. Took our tea. A most marvellous view. Storm clouds, shafts of timorous golden sunlight, the glittering Severn, a vast expanse of green and pleasant countryside, the towers of Gloucester Cathedral and Welsh mountains.

22 Monday
The *Nark* is progressing favourably complete with illustrations by Perg. Scarcely anyone or anything is immune from biting satire and several of the more prominent members of the Staff would sue us for libel if they saw our 'mag' [A mixture of schoolboy and journalist hyperbole. Only two copies extant, the original and one copied out by Syd]. Cricket this morning ... I had one rotten ball, dead on the middle peg which I hit for 3 and then stumps were drawn. Curse. Have written to Margaret accepting invitation.

23 Tuesday
Rugby Touch competition for the Upper School started this morning. My team on paper does not look too good but we managed to beat Archer's crew 3-1 and win our way into the second round, which is to be played off tomorrow morning. Four of us played tennis on the court all evening. Perg had gone to train the L.D.V.* So Davies came on my side, against Ras and Syd. They won the first set 6-4, we the second 8-6 and the third was a draw 1-1 when bad light stopped play. Most enjoyable but more Rugby Touch tomorrow. [*L.D.V. i.e. Local Defence Volunteers – this organisation began life in mid May. Of course, wags had it that L.D.V. really signified Look Duck Vanish. In a few weeks this volunteer defence force would be re-designated – Home Guard. For some years HGS had run an O.T.C. – Officer Training Corps in which Perg became a sergeant.]

24 Wednesday
Yippee! Succeeded in reaching the semi-finals in the Rugby Touch competition ... I was forced to play a little more vigorously due to Merry's bear like tactics and bull like rushes. Was cautioned and penalised about six times. Went to Mrs Wheatleys to tea. Amy there. They treated us right royally and Mrs W nearly broke down when we said goodbye. Good kind dear old soul. One of the best and one fine upstanding woman whom I shall never recall to mind without feeling a deep sense of gratitude and admiration.

P.11.

Antithesis.
    "I'm twice the man on bread and jam".
    "I'm nearly dead on jam and bread."

How to pitch a tent.
                Heat pitch until it melts then apply with
a brush.

Imaginary conversation between two Northfieldites.
A & B.

  A. – ' Hiyah.'
  B. – ' Ther.'
  A. — ' Wot I says is like this 'ere. These b—
Germans ought to blasted orf the face of the earth,
that's wot I says.'
  B. — ' Admitted, but, we must draw the line
somewhere.'
  A. — ' Garn, wivout a word of a lie I can honestly
say they kills the blokes and eats 'em.'
  B. — ' Even so we must exercise judicious mercy.'
  A. — ' Bilge, let's have a bolsch.'
  B. — ' Oko-doke I'm ready for a rant.'

Above and next page: Extracts from *The Nark.*

FEED YOUR FRIENDS ON —:·········

PAINS
PURE
PINK
SAUSAGES

THEY DEFY
DESTRUCTION

P.13.

POPULAR SCIENCE.

    We have great pleasure in publishing the full report of Professor P. KIN's recent research in the field of science. It will be recalled that the professor is world famous for his discovery of a cheap substitute for water.

    "Potato Plast"

    "While dining off potatoe pie and potatoe in the Stroud Canteen, Bedford St, I was suddenly seized with the idea of converting the potatoe surplus into a new material for industry. After months of strenuous research I have at last perfected the revolutionary plastic, "Potatoplast." Its advantages will be readily appreciated when one considers the remarkable cheapness and plentiful supply of the raw material. When under test it was found that the new plastic possessed remarkable elasticity, durability, malleability and ductility. Among its manifold uses may be included the facts that it:- can be carried in the pocket and chewed at will, can be used to cure coughs, colds and corns, as plastic wood and for sundry culinary

P.14.

purposes. It also makes an excellent hot poultice and as a glue there is none its equal."

    "Ferro-concrete"

    "At the same establishment later in the meal? [semi-concious] my tortured stomach was called upon to suffer further indignities viz. tombstone and rhubarb — Hastily purchasing the whole consignment I speedily took out a patent and soon found a ~~product~~ market for my new product in the paving stone industry. The S.U.D.C now have the monopoly."

    This is a condensation of the actual report, highly technical details having been omitted.

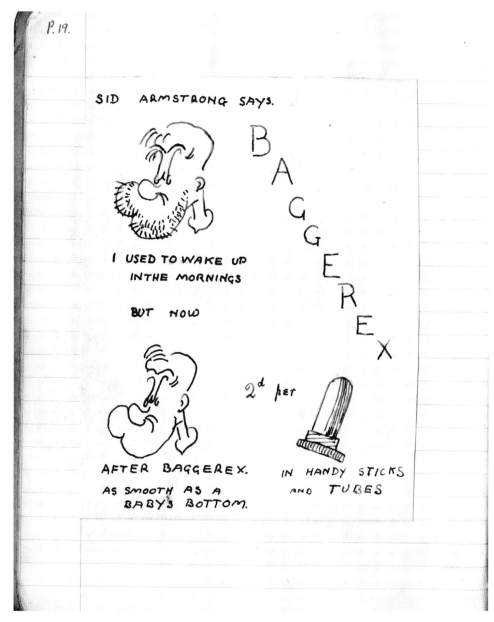

Extracts from *The Nark*.

Mr and Mrs A. Lindon, splendid foster-parents, remembered with admiration and affection.

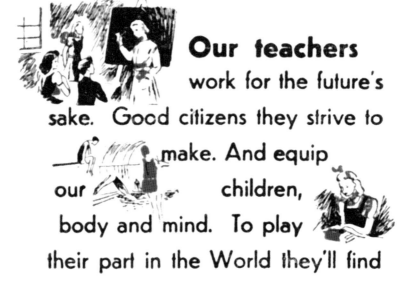

A fitting tribute to the sterling work teachers do.

D Dann, Barrett, Thompson.
2) Modely, Sanders, Deeley Forster,
3) Hayward, Burton, Bendall, Potter,
Mr Lindon, Rees, Mckenzie, Kent, Escott, Bendall,
Heath, Griffiths, Hood, Stroud,

Northfield 1940.

H.L.S, Pigott, Davies, Millichip, Heath,
Saunders, Davenport, Burnell.
Anderson, Armstrong, Mrs. Pritchard, Mrs. Lindon,
4). Blakemore, Saint, Startin, Deakin, Seers, Grainger, Peakin, Viggers,
Walters, Swinfern, Quanta.

Bingo! Full House.

25 Thursday

Sent all my luggage off in advance. Cost 4/-. Most busy and hectic time. Went to town with Syd and Perg. Bought presents for Mom, Dad & Bryan [a young nephew] also Mr & Mrs Lindon and Mrs Pritchard. [Housekeeper of no nonsense calibre who had replaced Phyllis.] Had a haircut. Final reports issued in the afternoon. Mine quite good. Excellent testimonial from the Head. Shook hands with him and was wished the best of luck. This is the worst part of school life saying goodbye, especially as I have made so many friends. No longer shall I be able to say 'coming out for half an hour?' etc. It's going to be a big jolt to break away from all these affectionate ties. We lost to Marling School at cricket. Had supper with the rest of the gang and Davies with Mr and Mrs Lindon. Reminiscences. At tea-time I had made the presentation. Another excellent testimonial from Baggy.

26 Friday

Set off early this morning and soon arrived at Gloucester where Dennis and I caught a local train to Worcester. Rotten having to say goodbye to one's pals. Hope we can arrange reunions. Arrived at Margaret's home at half 1. Met Margaret. Got to go to school all aft. Sent me a telegram this morning but it failed to reach me in time. Glad it didn't. Mrs D and the aunt and uncle treated me very kindly and

Stroud Station. Even today it has changed very little.

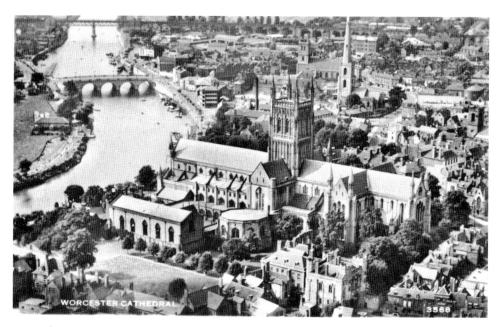

Worcester cathedral.

By the time we left Stroud, this well known landmark, like all signposts throughout the country had vanished because of the threat of invasion. So where now?

Location? Slight puzzle, soon solved. Memories were suitably refreshed during the post war period.

I am certain that I made a favourable impression. Went rowing in the afternoon and again with Margaret in the evening. How pleasant it is to be in her company. Leaning out of the carriage window to say goodbye the whistle went and our lips met as of mutual accord. All cares and anxieties melted away. Returned my blown kiss as the train steamed out. Words cannot express my feelings of joy and exhilaration. Uplifted. Arrived home late but happy with another invitation.

EPILOGUE

The impact of war on the life of the school from 1939 to 1945 was far more drastic than it had been from 1914 to 1918. The fear of large-scale air-raids had made the Government decide that all school children should be evacuated from the main industrial centres. Consequently, on 1 September 1939, the day Germany invaded Poland and two days before Britain declared war on Germany, boys were recalled to school from their summer holidays and taken by train to Stroud in Gloucestershire. For the next two years the headquarters of Handsworth Grammar School was the Marling School, Stroud.

Most of the boys were billeted with private householders in Stroud, though some fifty boys were accommodated in a large empty house which the school took over under the supervision of Mr and Mrs Lindon. This sudden uprooting of boys from their familiar surroundings, most of them being separated from their parents for the first time, inevitably brought problems, problems that were of a constant of course increased as food rationing made the feeding of hungry boys a constant anxiety. That these problems were so speedily solved represents a great tribute to the kindliness and forbearance of the foster-mothers of Stroud. Tribute must also be paid to those staff wives who assisted so nobly in looking after the boys' physical, medical and moral welfare.

The education of the boys continued as normally as was possible, though with two schools sharing one building a 'shift' system had to be introduced so that most of the academic lessons took place in the afternoons with the mornings devoted to physical activities. Social activities proved difficult to organise, but a few football and cricket matches were arranged, the O.T.C. continued to function, and the School Choir gave extracts from Handel's Creation at Stroud Parish Church. Church Services were arranged for the boys every Sunday morning at the Parish Church.

[History book excerpt.]

ALSO AVAILABLE FROM AMBERLEY PUBLISHING

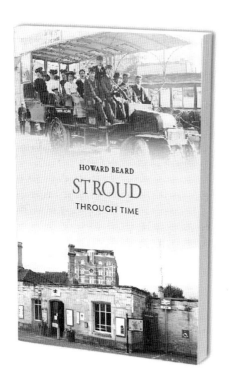

Stroud Through Time
Howard Beard
ISBN: 978-1-84868-039-5

Minchinhampton & Amberley Through Time
Howard Beard
ISBN: 978-1-84868-047-0

Nailsworth & Woodchester Through Time
Howard Beard
ISBN: 978-1-84868-050-0

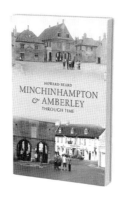

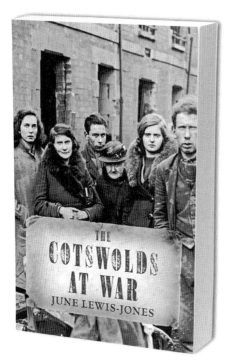

The Cotswolds at War
June Lewis-Jones
ISBN: 978-1-84868-362-4

A detailed account of what life was like for evacuees in the Cotswolds.

Available from all good bookshops
or to order direct please call
01285-760-030
www.amberley-books.com